PRAISE FOR

EQUINE THERAPY EXPOSED

Meg Kirby has truly lifted the lid on the inner workings of equine assisted psychotherapy and learning, an area that has often received little attention and understanding in the public domain and academic literature. In particular, a fascinating insight is provided into the experiential method that underpins The Equine Psychotherapy Institute's successful model. Through this book, one is able to gain a deeper knowledge of how the client, practitioner, horse, and environment subtly interact to influence the conduct of therapeutic sessions. A strongly client-centered approach is evident throughout the broad variety of case study discussions, highlighting the vast array of clients who may benefit from this innovative approach to health and wellbeing.

Carlie J. Driscoll, PhD
Associate Professor & Director
University of Queensland Animal-Assisted Interventions Alliance

Equine Therapy Exposed is a valuable resource for anyone interested in a real-life glimpse into the EAP/EAL process taught by The Equine Psychotherapy Institute. This book beautifully illustrates the power and effectiveness of the EAP/EAL process, and how it supports new opportunities and choices for relationship and emotional growth. In the unique case studies presented, each one demonstrates the co-creative process between the practitioner, client and horses, and how moving into contact and connection provides the foundation for profound healing and change. This book will inspire you!

Joan Rieger, MA, LPC
Director of the Gestalt Institute of the Rockies & Gestalt Equine Psychotherapist

Meg Kirby has written a dynamic and valuable book that provides readers with a unique glimpse on how she has learned to apply equine therapy services at her Institute. The book is filled with tremendous insights and practical suggestions. I believe that this book would be immensely helpful to professionals attempting to work alongside horses to support their clients' wellbeing.

Aubrey H. Fine Ed.D. Professor Emeritus
CA Poly State University, Licensed Psychologist
Editor of The Handbook on Animal Assisted Therapy

Meg Kirby's Equine Therapy Exposed is an outstanding book for beginners as well as experienced equine assisted therapy practitioners. The case studies are rich and varied. The practice points and comments are very helpful in illustrating specific aspects of equine assisted psychotherapy. Equally, this text is a fantastic resource for integrating psychotherapy with a range of somatic and nature-based therapies, not just equine therapy. The AWARE Therapy TM model is highly innovative, weaving together seminal psychotherapeutic approaches with eastern wisdom and meditative traditions – Meg is a woman after my own heart!

Melissa O'Shea, PhD
Clinical Psychologist, Academic and Yoga Teacher,
Master of Clinical Leadership (MCL), Deakin University

Equine Therapy Exposed, by Meg Kirby, takes a significant and meaningful step in the advancement of the professionalization of the fields of Equine-Assisted Psychotherapy and Equine-Assisted Learning. Presenting a model which she has developed (EPI Model and AWARE Therapy TM), that takes advantage of mechanisms unique to these two fields, Kirby is actually showing the reader an approach as opposed to a manual. This distinction is critical in that it allows for flexibility that focuses on the needs of any given client, at any given point in time, as opposed to focusing on rules to be followed. The case studies splendidly help the reader understand both the depth and the processes that can be achieved in psychotherapy and in learning, with the help of the integration of equines into the setting, through the use of this approach.

Nancy Parish-Plass, MA Social Work and Certified in Advanced Psychotherapy Studies
Founding and Current Chairperson of IAAAP
Israeli Association of Animal-Assisted Psychotherapy

If you are interested in how to work relationally with horses in a psychotherapy and learning context, this book clearly outlines The Equine Psychotherapy Institute's methodology and provides case studies to illustrate how the theory underpins practice. The AWARE Therapy™ model provides a clear framework for practitioners to embrace the Gestalt foundations of here-and-now, embodied relationships. As a follow-up to her first book, An Introduction to Equine Assisted Psychotherapy: Principles Theory and Practice of the Equine Psychotherapy Institute Model, this book showcases the adaptability of the approach to a wide range of client populations and highlights the importance of allowing each session to organically emerge through the relationships between practitioner, horse, and client.

Veronica Lac, Ph D
Executive Director
The HERD Institute®, USA

As the involvement of equines and other species in psychotherapy becomes more popular, resources are increasing dramatically. Many focus on the benefits to humans without delineation of the theoretical principles underpinning the approach or consideration of the animals' experience. It is refreshing to read a volume that highlights these critical factors while telling the human story as well. Meg Kirby's edited volume, Equine Therapy Exposed, does just that. She and the contributing authors have created a readable, well-organized, and compelling book that starts with a grounding in Kirby's AWARE™ Therapy's principles and concepts, and follows with case studies that provide depth of understanding of core therapeutic principles applied with a diverse range of presenting concerns and clients. In particular, I appreciate the focus on acceptance, not only to foster the client's awareness and journey through the experiential process, but also of the horses, respecting them as the unique and individual sentient beings that they are. Thorough elucidation of therapeutic processes when animals are involved remains relatively uncommon in the literature. Brava to Meg Kirby and contributors for creating this most helpful exploration of just that!

--Risë VanFleet, PhD, RPT-S, CDBC, CAEBC/I
Coauthor with Tracie Faa-Thompson of the award-winning *Animal Assisted Play Therapy*
Principal, International Institute for Animal Assisted Play Therapy

"We deeply accept the otherness of clients as they are – the way we accept a tree as it is, in all its uniqueness and beauty."

MEG KIRBY

EQUINE THERAPY EXPOSED

REAL LIFE CASE STUDIES OF EQUINE ASSISTED
PSYCHOTHERAPY AND EQUINE ASSISTED LEARNING WITH
EVERYDAY PEOPLE AND HORSES

MEG KIRBY

Equine Therapy Exposed

First published in Australia 2021 by Meg Kirby.

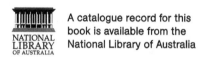

A catalogue record for this book is available from the National Library of Australia

ISBN: 978-0-6450621-0-6

Author: Meg Kirby

Title: Equine Therapy Exposed: Real Life Case Studies of Equine Assisted Psychotherapy and Equine Assisted Learning with Everyday People and Horses

Subject: Equine Assisted Therapy, Equine Assisted Psychotherapy, Horse Therapy, Animal Assisted Therapy, Animal Assisted Psychotherapy

DISCLAIMER

The material in this publication is of the nature of general comment only and does not represent professional advice. It is not intended to provide specific guidance for particular circumstances and should not be relied on as the basis for any decision to take action or not take action on any matters it covers. Readers should obtain professional advice as appropriate before taking any action. To the maximum extent permitted by law, the author and publisher disclaim all responsibility and liability to any person, arising directly or indirectly from any person taking or not taking action based on the information in this book.

Cover design, interior design and layout: Amy De Wolfe | amydewolfe.com
Cover photography: Renata Apanaviciene | renata.photography

DEDICATION

I dedicate this book to Crystal, who is the queen of feelings, expression, boundaries, authenticity, letting-go, and going back to grazing.

Ever since she graced my paddock in all her chestnut hair, flaxen-mane glory, she was all-woman, all-in, and yet so gentle, patient and kind to me and many humans she has encountered.

The bio-feedback Crystal offers is nothing less than superb. I trust her implicitly now. After 18 years of being in relationship, we have developed a great deal of trust and open communication together.

Crystal is my "queen", my mentor and my friend, and such an amazing support for people of all ages, stages, gender and uniqueness who have the good fortune to meet and learn with her.

Thank you, Crystal, I love you so much, words are nowhere near enough for us. Your presence is everywhere in my life, whether I am in the paddock with you or not...I will stay attuned to your teachings.

Meg Kirby

ACKNOWLEDGEMENTS

I wish to acknowledge all the amazing students I have had the opportunity to teach, be with, and learn from over the last 10 years at the Institute. You continue to teach me so much about relationship and what it takes to be a trusted leader, trainer and colleague. I am becoming a better practitioner, teacher and trainer because of you!

Our contact has not always been easy, of course, it has been disturbing at times, like all good awareness and authentic relationship. My experience training and mentoring you has led to continual developments of our EPI Model, and, in myself as a person.

For this, I thank you all. We have, together, developed a rich and wonderful community of practitioners across the globe, dedicated to professional excellence and heartfelt connection.

May our EPI herd of practitioners continue to grow and develop together, as well as inspire wellbeing for all humans, horses, animals, and the natural world, where we are privileged to live.

Meg Kirby

CONTENTS

Chapter 1:
INTRODUCTION

My mission in writing and compiling this book was to give you, the reader, a real-life insight into what is known to the layperson as 'equine therapy' yet is actually, Equine Assisted Psychotherapy or Equine Assisted Learning.

Specifically, my mission is to offer a unique exposé into *what is Equine Assisted Psychotherapy (EAP) and Equine Assisted Learning (EAL)*, and, *what can happen with diverse clients* in EAP and EAL sessions (which we teach at The Equine Psychotherapy Institute).

This is so important on many levels.

Firstly, it can support the general public's understanding of the *potential impact and power of equine assisted and animal assisted therapy* (with well-trained practitioners).

Secondly, it showcases the diverse clients' presenting issues and needs, and the different ways of working with supporting client change with horses, *that all have clear theory and practice methodology foundations.*

Thirdly, it provides an *insight into the unique psychotherapy mechanisms* at play in this innovative, experiential therapeutic methodology of EAP, and the unique experiential learning techniques in EAL.

Finally, it showcases *the unique AWARE Therapy™ approach that we teach at The Equine Psychotherapy*

I trust you will enjoy the journey, reading and feeling into the sessions, and reflecting on the theory and practice, the key ingredients that support client change.

Institute (EPI), which underpins EAP and EAL sessions. Our theory and practice are founded heavily in contemporary humanistic psychotherapy approaches including relational gestalt psychotherapy, alongside somatic and brain-based trauma-informed practices, specifically somatic experiencing and polyvagal theory. It also integrates my unique take on *Horse Wisdom* – the wisdom that horses' model about relationship, wellbeing and healthy self-regulation.

I developed The Equine Psychotherapy Institute (EPI) model in 2011, and our training Institute has become well known around Australia, and now across many other countries including New Zealand, Canada, Poland, Sweden, England and Singapore. Our recent Online EAP and EAL training has allowed students from all around the world to access our training and become a part of our international *herd of practitioners.*

Although EAP and EAL practitioners offer a different facilitation process, which is reflected in the different scope of practice of EAP and EAL, practitioners are taught a lot of overlapping theory and practice that ensures client safety and horse safety are paramount.

To be clear, EAP's (also referred to as EAT's – equine assisted therapists) must be qualified and registered mental health professionals including psychologists, social workers, psychotherapists, counsellors, credentialed mental health nurses and specialist trained mental health occupational therapists. These professionals are governed by their respective peak body, and have done substantial additional training, supervision and assessment in equine assisted psychotherapy.

Equine Assisted Learning practitioners have specific training in equine assisted learning which may include educational, social-emotional learning, personal development and professional learning (i.e. team building and leadership) skills and competencies. EAL's are not necessarily qualified professionals or members of a peak governing body.

Many EAL's are qualified teachers, life coaches, riding coaches, and organisational consultants, governed by their respective peak professional body. It is always important for consumers to know the qualifications, training and experience of their equine assisted practitioner, and we expect transparency and ethical professionalism from all our practitioners.

I reached out to some of our wonderful EPI certified practitioners with an offer to contribute a case study in this exposé on EAP and EAL, and was delighted to receive some rich, varied and skilful examples of our EPI work.

I trust you will enjoy the journey, reading and feeling into the sessions, and reflecting on the theory and practice, the key ingredients that support client change. Each chapter is authored by an individual EPI Practitioner. The comment boxes are authored by myself (Meg Kirby, as founder of The EPI model and Aware Therapy) and offer the reader an opportunity for further insight, reflection and a deeper understanding of the work.

I have continued to further develop the EPI approach over the 10 years since its original inception as the *first Australian model* of EAP and EAL. It has blossomed into an internationally renowned, therapeutically sophisticated, trauma-informed and deeply ethical approach to equine assisted practice that transforms people's and horses' lives. Our advanced, specialist training programs now include animal assisted psychotherapy and nature assisted psychotherapy. We are proud to be the first training organisation in Australia to be teaching at a postgraduate equivalent level in equine assisted psychotherapy. I, and the Institute, have recently received some fantastic news that our Australian peak regulating body for Counselling and Psychotherapy, PACFA (Psychotherapy and Counselling Federation of Australia), has granted specialist accreditation to our Equine Assisted Psychotherapy training for 2021 and beyond. PACFA has confirmed that our training is assessed and accredited as AQF Level 8 (Australian Qualification Framework/ AQF levels criteria indicate the relative complexity and /or depth of achievement and the autonomy required to demonstrate that achievement. Level 1 has the lowest level of complexity and Level 10 has the highest). Our Equine Assisted Psychotherapy training is the highest level of education in animal and equine assisted psychotherapy available across Australia. We are extremely proud of the high ethical and professional standards we maintain, and we will continue to lead the way in world-class education in equine assisted psychotherapy, animal assisted psychotherapy and nature assisted psychotherapy for the future.

I am ever-grateful for all that I have learned and continue to learn from our diverse group of talented students and practitioners (over 340 students have studied with us during this first decade of training at the Institute), and, from our most precious herd of horses – Crystal, Stormy, Image, Alirah, Lily, Star, Raj, Amir, Ashaar, River, Lexy and Jensen.

Thank you!

Meg Kirby

PLEASE NOTE: I am not showcasing examples of EAT that include physiotherapy, occupational therapy or speech therapy as the dominant therapy. EAP differs from these forms of equine assisted therapy, in that *the focus is on providing counselling or psychotherapy,* not physiotherapy (physical therapy), speech therapy or occupational therapy with horses.

The mental health clinicians trained in EAP offer a counselling or psychotherapeutic intervention, with appropriate counselling or psychotherapy 'therapeutic goals' as the primary focus for the intervention.

We are also not showcasing *Therapeutic Riding,* as this is a different intervention and approach to both EAP and EAL. We do not teach equine assisted physiotherapy, speech therapy, occupational therapy or therapeutic riding at the Institute.

We recommend reading *"The Clinical Practice of Equine Assisted Therapy"* by Leif Hallberg for a more comprehensive overview of the range of EAT (including EAP) and other equine based interventions available around the world.

" Awareness is the
road less travelled. "

MEG KIRBY

Chapter 2
HOW TO MAKE SENSE OF
THE SESSIONS

T his book introduces and gives an overview of the AWARE Therapy™ approach that underpins the EPI Model and equine sessions you are about to read. This way, you can reflect upon
the sessions and begin to sharpen and deepen your understanding of this unique practice
approach taught at The Equine Psychotherapy Institute.

This will be very helpful as you read the case study material in the body of the book and engage with the material in the comment boxes. The comment boxes include further insight, reflection and feedback from founder of the model, Meg Kirby. This is designed to support your curiosity and deepen your understanding of this innovative equine assisted practice approach.

AWARE Therapy™

AWARE Therapy™ is a unique therapy approach developed as a *specialist* equine, animal, and nature assisted psychotherapy approach. The Aware Therapy™ approach underpins all teaching, training, and practice at The Equine Psychotherapy Institute (2011-2020) in Equine Assisted Psychotherapy, Equine Assisted Learning, Animal Assisted Psychotherapy, Animal Assisted Learning, Nature Assisted Psychotherapy and Nature Assisted Learning, training and practices. Meg Kirby developed AWARE Therapy™ as a unique psychotherapeutic synthesis of Relational Gestalt Therapy, Mindfulness Psychotherapy, Buddhist Psychotherapy, Cognitive Behavioural Therapy, Neuroscience, Trauma informed approaches including Somatic Experiencing, combined with *Wisdom* teachings and the support of horses, animals and the natural world. The 10 *theoretical and practice focuses* articulate the AWARE Therapy™ approach.

AWARE Therapy™ - 10 THEORY AND PRACTICE PRINCIPLES INCLUDE:

A 1. **Awareness**

W 2. **Wisdom**

A   **Approach - of Horses, Animals and Nature**

R 3. **Relationship** 4. **Regulation** 5. **Resourcing**

E 6. **Experiential** 7.**Experimental** 8.**Embodiment** 9.**Ethical** 10.**Enrichment**

INTRODUCTION TO AWARE Therapy™

1. AWARENESS

Awareness is the goal, and the phenomenological method of inquiry and observation is the method, which facilitates this goal in all EPI Model sessions. Awareness practice is woven through the entire fabric of the EPI Model EAP and EAL sessions, from the safety guideline, to the regulation and resourcing exercises, to the equine experiences, to the inquiry and deepening processing, to the integration and closure facilitation skills.

All sessions are designed to support clients to begin to become aware of their whole experience (including their body-emotion-cognitive-behavioural-relational layers of experience), in a manner that suits the individual client. Clients are also supported (where appropriate) to become aware of patterns that one was previously unaware of (i.e. unconscious patterns and processes).

Practitioners track the client's perspective and projections to step into the client's world, engage with the existing level of awareness, and slowly support expanding the client's awareness, as appropriate.

With awareness practice (noticing, feeling into, and welcoming our experience, as *it is* rather than as it 'should' be or seeking the 'ideal' experience), one is changed. The paradoxical theory of change underpins our awareness practice with clients. This theory and practice supports a turning towards our experience 'as it is', rather than trying to change, improve or fix the behaviour with a solution. It is this important paradigm shift (moving away from solution-focused and 'ideal self' improvements, towards, accepting and inquiring into our actual experience), that all practitioners are invited to make personally, before professionally inviting clients to do the same. Moving away from layperson 'problem solving' approaches and solution-focused counselling or psychologically based orientations towards change can be very difficult at first!

This *here and now practice* orientation forms a large part of the work throughout the entire session, which is woven through awareness exercises, grounding exercises, relational experiences with the horses, and processing and integration facilitation stages. Clients, depending on their developmental age and stage, may be reflecting on this awareness process or they may not, as appropriate to the capacity and needs of the client.

Given that awareness practice is inherently activating for clients, practitioners bring their trauma-informed lens and interventions into play as needed, to keep clients emotionally secure and safe from re-traumatisation.

PHENOMENOLOGICAL PRACTICE

Phenomenological practice supports practitioners to track the clients' subjective experience in the self-horse-practitioner-field relationship. It offers a non-interpretational approach, utilising skills in bracketing, describing, open and spacious curiosity and exploration – tracking all layers of a client's experience (including somatic, emotional, cognitive, behavioural, and relational experience).

This requires the practitioner to be very intentional and skilful in not assuming, generalising, interpreting or making meaning of a client's experience. The overall goal is to increase the client's awareness and choice of their own emerging 'figures of interest' or themes (i.e. feelings, needs, yearnings, patterns, values, desires and process), not the practitioner's emerging 'figures of interest'. This practice ensures the session is 'client-focused' and 'client-driven' and not directed by the practitioner's agenda, hypotheses, theory and unconscious processes.

2. WISDOM APPROACH – UTILISING THE WISDOM OF HORSES

HORSES AS CHANGE AGENTS

AWARE Therapy™ includes orienting to, experiencing, relating with, and learning from, horses, other animals and nature as a fundamental part of the theory of change and practice methodology. A fundamental part of the model, therefore, is learning with horses, and, learning from horses. Learning with horses means that practitioners are tracking how the horse or herd engages with each client, tracking how the horse's presence, non-verbal response, relationship, touch, engagement and uniqueness impacts the client and the client's experience of themselves, others, relationship and life. There are no expectations for the horses to respond in any particular way.

For example, horses are not asked to be calm, do what the client asks or wants, or follow any traditional agenda of a 'horsemanship', 'horse-person-ship' or riding setting. Practitioners have an agenda of safety to ensure the horses and clients are safe (unharmed physically or psychologically) but that is where the agenda ends.

Practitioners want the horse to be who they are, share what they feel and want, and behave in a way that is authentic and expressive for them (as long as the client is safe). The practitioner's job is to track the key ingredients the horse is offering in that unique encounter, that contribute to client change.

Practitioners are taught about the ways the horses can contribute to client change, but practitioners and clients are always invited to be openly curious about *what is actually happening*, and the experience and meaning this has for the client. Practitioners must bring openness, and curiosity, with no agenda for the horse/s to behave and contribute in any specific way, in order to track what the horse is doing and how the experience unfolds for the client.

Below are some examples of how horses can become agents of change, that we teach practitioners at The Equine Psychotherapy Institute.

HORSE AS CHANGE AGENT - THE HORSE AS:

Client (Self)	client projection onto the horse, so the horse in this moment becomes the client, or an extension of the client
Client (Other)	client projection onto the horse, where the projection is of a significant other from the clients' history (referred to as transference)
Co-Regulator	regulating the clients' nervous system. The horse's large and settled physiology acts as a co-regulator, supporting the client's nervous system to regulate
Unique Feedback	bio-feedback mechanism and equine behavioural response to clients offers data about how client impacts others

Role Model	modelling to client's healthy ways of behaving i.e. living in the present rather than the past (in one's mind or story)
Emotional Safety and Trust	the safe, non-judgemental other (horse) supports safety and stress reduction in the physiology and psychology of the client
Engagement, Motivation, Interest and Catalyst	supporting clients' attendance and further engagement, interest and motivation in personal exploration and change
Education Support	being in relationship with horses can teach clients about many things i.e. taking responsibility for meeting others' needs and caring for others
Evocative Cue or Trigger	the horse's presence triggers present or past feelings and/or supports an activation in clients. Here, the horse may also represent the unsafe other or be a catalyst, evoking unprocessed emotional and psychological material
Safe Attachment	the horse provides the human with an experience of attachment needs, such as, safe Movement, Touch, Holding (and the client may experience a *corrective experience*)
Nature	the horse provides a literal and metaphoric doorway for clients in meeting biophilic needs (to feel and be connected with the natural world, and themselves, as nature)
Authentic Relationship	an honest and direct relational other
Non-judgemental and Accepting Other, providing Confirmation	here the client experiences feeling *seen, heard and valued* – loved – by another being. This may include an oxytocin download
Challenging Other	the horse's behaviour, presence or movements provide a new and novel experience to negotiate, think through or contemplate, which stimulates problem solving, creativity, responding to the current field, and other skills that together build overall health and resilience.

Clients can engage with horses at Liberty (free with room to move independently without any tack), On-line (horses are haltered and attached to a lead-rope) and in Led-Mounted Sessions (horses are haltered on lead rope, the client is safely mounted, and the practitioner facilitates the clients therapeutic or learning goals at a halt or walk).

EPI HORSE WISDOM PROGRAM®

The Institute has trademarked a unique 7 session psycho-educational Horse Wisdom Program® that teaches clients about the wisdom of horses. We bring an engaging approach where the practitioners teach social-emotional skills through talking about *what horses already do*. In this way we view the horses as our teachers (alongside, experiencing and learning in relationship with horses).

3. RELATIONSHIP – HORSE-CLIENT-PRACTITIONER LENS

The practitioner's interest is in offering the opportunity for clients to *experience* relationship, *learn* in relationship and openly *explore* relationship, with horses, and the practitioner themselves. The relationship becomes the "live experiment" that clients utilise to experience safe, mutually beneficial, and aware relationship.

This relational and experiential focus is inherent in the approach, and is something that is a highly valued part of the model's theory of change, in line with the Common Factors Theory on relationship as an important and (common) component or predictor of client outcome.

Common Factors Theory proposes that different theoretical and evidence-based approaches to psychotherapy and counselling have common components, and that those components account for outcome, more than components that are unique to each approach.[1]

4. & 5. REGULATION, RESOURCING AND TRAUMA-INFORMED PRACTICES

The focus is to ensure that clients with trauma histories (whether it be PTSD, complex trauma or developmental trauma) are supported to regulate their nervous system, track their window of tolerance and activation-deactivation cycles to ensure that the processes of awareness-building, growth, relationship exploration and insight are not just tolerable, but able to be integrated.

Practitioners bring an intention to build the clients' overall resources, including both inner-supports and outer-supports, over the duration of both EAP and EAL sessions. This part of the practice includes sensory, somatic, cognitive and behavioural interventions tailored to each client and their needs.

6. & 7. EXPERIENTIAL AND EXPERIMENTAL PRACTICE

The experiential approach brings a focus on learning and healing through experiencing, rather than *talking through* or *talking about*. Here, practitioners invite clients to notice what is happening, as they are experiencing it, to increase awareness and connection, and to illuminate patterns and choices. The experimental approach ensures practitioners do not get stuck in a formula or agenda that suits them,

[1]Imel,Z., & Wampold, B. (2008). *The Importance of Treatment and the Science of Common Factors in Psychotherapy. Handbook of Counselling Psychology*, (4th ed.). (pp. 249-262): John Wiley & Sons Inc.

but not their client! Practitioners are trained to design and utilise experiments, that they offer to their client to heighten awareness and foster relationship, resources and sense of self. These relationally-oriented experiments with horses, practitioner and the natural environment, support growth and change via experiencing, exploring and becoming curious.

The client-focused approach requires practitioners to be aware, responsive and creative in the here and now, to offer a "new experience" and "experiment" that is uniquely placed to support awareness, growth and change for each *individual client* or client system.

This approach looks to resource, support, nourish and facilitate the client's experience and journey in a way that honours the innate wisdom and capacity the client has to reach their potential and grow, if they have enough inner and outer supports and relational resources available.

Practitioners look to provide, metaphorically, the water, the soil, the fertiliser, and the container to nourish the client to do what they can innately do (and need to do) to grow, mature and reach their full potential. This trust in the client's wisdom and potential to grow and change is an important value and attitude of the EPI practitioner.

8. EMBODIMENT PRACTICE

AWARE Therapy™ brings a *somatic lens* to the awareness, relationship, wisdom-oriented and ex-perimental approach, supporting an *immediacy practice* where the client is asked to track their body sensations, felt sense and inner experience (as it is emerging, shifting and changing in the here and now, with the practitioner and the horses). The client is able to differentiate (put words to and give attention to), the different layers of their experience and how they may be impacting the whole client. Focusing on sensations, rather than just thoughts or feelings or behaviours, allows clients to notice what is *most true*, in any moment of experience, giving them more insight, awareness, choice and a deeper connection to their whole self. Young clients or adult clients are supported to do so in a trauma-informed and appropriate way (i.e. tracking what is tolerable for them, developmentally appropriate, and useful at a particular time). This somatic and embodied approach is something the horses' model beautifully, living in their bodies in a connected and integrated way, which can become a great resource and support for clients over time.

9. ETHICAL LENS

The emotional and physical safety of our clients and our horses is paramount in the EPI practice and AWARE Therapy™ approach. Practitioners agree to abide by our EPI Code of Ethics that serve to protect clients and horses. Alongside their focus on client safety, practitioners look for the horse's consent, tracking their communications, non-verbal and verbal behaviour every moment in session, looking to maintain and prioritise the horses' wellbeing and welfare.

The EPI Model believes the horses' wellbeing and welfare is paramount to the clients' wellbeing and welfare, and to the horses themselves. If a client intentionally or unintentionally attempts to harm the horse, this becomes the focus for the practitioner's intervention. That way the ethics become part of the intervention. Now this rarely happens, but even with subtle degrees of discomfort or no consent, the practitioner is interested in raising inquiry around, "I wonder what the horse is feeling right now?" (as it is appropriate and developmentally appropriate for each client.)

All practitioners learn about the *I-Thou* relational approach with horses (I-Thou Horse-person-ship™, as taught by Meg Kirby) and this forms the foundations of the ethical stance (behind the scenes, outside and inside of sessions). Practitioners must look to *feel into* the horse's subjective experience, body and orientation, be present and not in a role, bring an intention to appreciate the horse's uniqueness and inherent value as a sentient being, and, 'lean into' any difficulties, ruptures and conflict that may occur in the horse-practitioner relationship.

These attitudes and skills act as insurance during the equine assisted session for the welfare of the horse/s and offers an opportunity to deepen the equine-human client-practitioner-horse relationship, during session supporting client growth.

The I-Thou Horse-person-ship™ approach acts as the *ground* beneath which EAP and EAL sessions 'sit on'. These values and practices ensure practitioners never *use* the horse for the benefit of the client or themselves, nor objectify the horse as only a metaphor or canvas for the clients' projections.

Practitioners study equine studies and safe horsemanship in order to complete certification with EPI and are assessed on their understanding of the 'Five Freedoms' (created by the UK Farm Animal Welfare Council include the freedom from - hunger and thirst; discomfort; pain, injury or disease; fear and distress; and the freedom to express normal behaviour), horse care, horse management, and learning theory, among many other subjects. As an IAHAIO member (International Association Human-Animal Interactions Organisation), the Institute requires students to understand the One Health and One Welfare principles outlined in IAHAIO White Paper (2018) regarding understanding the interrelationship between animal welfare, human well-being and the environment.

The ethical orientation, equine studies, safe horsemanship and I-Thou Horse-person-ship™ sits as a solid foundation for practitioners to then choose particular horses, and particular equine experiences to offer clients, that will maximise safety for all, ensuring a rich growth, learning and healing opportunity in the context of equine assisted practice. The model openly values horses' freedom of expression, as well as teaching this to clients to support their own capacities for self-regulation, amongst many other skills.

In AWARE Therapy™ practitioners are always encouraged to reflect on the question (as an ethical compass) 'Is this (intervention) good for the horse? (or animal, nature, or natural environment, in the context of animal and nature assisted psychotherapy). The EPI code of ethics stipulates and guides practitioners to be oriented, always, around client safety, horse safety, and an ethical compass for all practice.

10. ENRICHMENT

Practitioners are intentionally reflecting on enrichment for the client- practitioner-horse-animals-nature system, in and out of session. There is a focus on what is safe and good (ethical and welfare focus) alongside a focus on what enriches the experience for the client-horse-natural environment interaction and experience. Many practitioners design experiments that intentionally enrich the horses' life and experience (e.g. going for a walk in the nearby bush or forest may be stimulating and nourishing for some horses, or, grazing at liberty in proximity to human clients enabling choice to engage at horses' free will), whilst meeting the therapeutic goals and enrichment needs (what feels interesting, stimulating and nurturing) for each unique client. Practitioners are also encouraged to reflect upon continually enriching the natural environment, bush, forest, country they are living, working or engaging with (e.g. planting out part of their properties with Indigenous trees or forest, building walking tracks for their horses' to minimise impact on the land, or using particular arenas or yards for herds to rest and rejuvenate so the land has a chance to rest and rejuvenate from the impact of hooves and grazing). This enrichment focus extends the ethical lens to include, "Is this good for the horse, is this good for the client, is this good for the land, is this good for me (as practitioner), and how can I further enrich us all?" Enrichment focuses on fostering stimulating environments that promote positive and nurturing expression in all humans, non-human species, and the wonderful ecology and ecological systems in which we all live.

OTHER THEORY AND PRACTICE SKILLS

ASSESSMENT

Here and Now Assessment and Context-History Assessment is an integral part of EAP sessions. Just as all psychotherapists and mental health practitioners engage in mental status examinations, crisis assessment and continual assessment of emerging themes, patterns, and needs in room-based settings, in the equine assisted setting, all these skills are continually utilised.

EAL practitioners engage in Here and Now assessments and carefully track the edges of their skills, competencies and scope of practice to keep their client safe and refer on to mental health practitioners or EAP's as needed.

DEVELOPMENTAL LENS

The EPI Model includes understanding the origins of patterns in attachment, core beliefs, behavioural patterns and other somatic, emotional and relational patterns –these patterns are called fixed creative adjustments.

This is where the client creatively adjusted to the early relational field they were born into (including caregiver/parenting-family-community-gender-cultural-political-environmental-international system). These "adjustments" become fixed over time, due to the significant function they may have played in survival, attachment and belonging for the infant or young person. These fixed creative adjustments include the cognitive-behavioural patterns that endure today in the form of symptoms, presenting problems, 'dysfunctional behaviour' or clinical diagnoses and disorders.

EAP's may work with the client's clinical diagnoses, tracking and exploring the fixed creative adjustments as they emerge during relationship with the horses and practitioner, and further exploring and processing the client's history and present experience.

EAL's do not explore fixed creative adjustments in the context of historical events and experience. However, EAL's may address many of these fixed cognitive-behavioural patterns as they arrive in the here and now, with the horses and the horse-human relationship.

All EPI practitioners understand that relationship patterns and self-development evolve through the course of infancy, childhood, adolescence and early adulthood, as intelligent protective mechanisms and work with these patterns through a developmental and field-oriented, relational lens, with the horses.

PRACTITIONER PERSONAL WORK

In the case studies, you will see how practitioners utilise bracketing, a particular skill in phenomenological practice, to notice, track, and contain *practitioner-as-self* thoughts and patterns that emerge in the context of EAP or EAL. These are noted by the practitioner, contained so they do not impact on the work with clients and are self-processed or addressed later in supervision or psychotherapy, as appropriate.

In AWARE Therapy™, practitioners understand field theory dictates that people will impact one another, that we are not separate beings, and that our inter-dependence and inter-connectedness mean that practitioners influence the client to greater or lesser degrees. Practitioners work with the lesser degrees through their own self-awareness practices, personal work commitment, bracketing and containing skills, and commitment to one's own psychotherapy and professional development in supervision and ongoing training.

Practitioners work to utilise bracketing to minimise influence on clients that is a hinderance and increase influence through a strong therapeutic alliance and relationship (with EAP's) and strong learning relationship (with EAL's). EPI practitioners' value personal work and view it as an integral part of building skills and competencies required in relationship-based interventions, such as EAP and EAL.

CREATIVITY AND CHOICE-POINTS

In a session, there are hundreds of possibilities and trajectories. Where the practitioner chooses to go with any client, what they say, don't say, how they orient, self-support, what equine experiences they offer, and how they track, follow the client's emergent themes, feelings, needs and behaviours will lead to an array of potential "choice-points."

These choice-points are not about better options, interventions, inquiry, observations or experiments. They are instances or moments in a session where there is a choice to be made. Practitioners always want to track the array of choice-points, to stay openly curious about other possibilities and options to attune and support client change.

Some practitioners openly refer to these in their thinking during a session or after session, and you will explore choice-points in this way, as you read and journey through these case studies. The EPI approach is to remain eternally openly curious, creative and reflective in practice.

SAFETY GUIDELINE

In the EPI approach, practitioners offer a specific safety guideline that supports clients to meet with the horses in a way that keeps them physically safe and psychologically safe by growing their capacity for awareness and self-governing. This serves as a psycho-educational support for clients. It provides literal support and equine information for clients to utilise whilst interacting with horses, who are inherently different to humans in species-related behaviour.

TRACKING EMERGENT THEMES AND PATTERNS

Practitioners track issues, themes, patterns, feelings, and needs that emerge for the client in the course of engagement with the horse, horses, or practitioner. Some clients will actively engage with these themes as they are developmentally capable. Other clients will not necessarily be in dialogue with the practitioner about these themes if the themes are outside their window of tolerance, developmentally inappropriate, or too early in the work for the relationship to sustain the challenging themes emerging.

The Here and Now assessment skills of the EPI practitioner ensure that they are tracking themes, bracketing where necessary, and processing those most likely of benefit to the client in the here and now.

PRACTITIONER AS "FELLOW TRAVELLER"

As mentioned in the previous section on experiments, creativity and the wisdom of the client, practitioners are looking to trust and follow the client's emerging wisdom. The practitioner orients within the professional relationship as a professional, 'fellow traveller' in that they are authentic, present, real, self-disclose only in service of the client, bracket and contain (their own agenda, impulses, needs and patterns) and offer a relational stance that 'leans into' any mis-attunements or ruptures in the professional alliance between client and practitioner (where attunement refers to sensing into others' feelings, emotions and mood and responding appropriately).

The practitioner is oriented as the expert on equine assisted *facilitation process* and *not* an expert on *client content! The client is viewed as the expert on themselves and their lives.*

This way, the practitioners are taught to develop presence, inclusion (feeling into the experience of the client), and confirmation (knowing the client is inherently valuable and not mistaking the clients for their own 'symptoms' or fixed creative adjustments).

Practitioners are trained to be very real, be themselves, and although skilful and perhaps masterful in their understanding and application of equine assisted theory and practice, to always be congruent and present.

Sometimes practitioners need to grade or calibrate the intensity of their capacity for presence and contact, so the client can remain inside their window of tolerance and not feel flooded or overwhelmed, given what they can manage in any intimate, albeit professional, encounter.

CONTACT STYLES AND INTROJECTS –
COGNITIVE-BEHAVIOURAL WORK

This has been addressed somewhat in the developmental lens section. As further support to understanding some of the case studies, it will be useful for the reader to understand that in Gestalt therapy theory, introjects can generally be understood as unaware, fixed beliefs, and contact styles, as relationship patterns. Contact styles commonly include retroflection, deflection, desensitisation, confluence, egotism (self-monitoring), introjection and projection.

EAP practitioners are working with the introject-contact style system (cognitive-behavioural patterns) that clients use with the horses (and themselves as practitioners), to understand the current unaware or unconscious patterns utilised. EAP practitioners explore the client's history to understand the origins, functions, purpose and context for the development of particular patterns that the client currently utilises as a part of self-organisation and relational function.

EAL's stay in the here and now (in their scope of practice) and process these patterns with the horses (not exploring the history, origins and function of the patterns). EAL's support the clients' expression in the here and now, and support clients to learn from the new, safe relationship experience, fostering new neural pathways to be developed (over time with repetition).

LEARNING GOALS AND THERAPEUTIC GOALS

A brief word on the importance of the Therapeutic Goals for EAP's and Learning Goals for EAL's and how they shape and dictate some of the process and session:

If a client presents with a want to explore and work on particular goals, yet, as the practitioner proceeds with the client session they notice that there are significant *emergent* themes and patterns that may change the clients' original goals, it is important to re-contract with the client (and parents of clients). This ensures transparency, effectiveness and that the service remains client-driven.

Soft contracting refers to when practitioners do this *verbally* within the main body of the session, as it is unfolding. This is addressed, clarified, and the client orients the practitioner around where they wish to focus for the remainder of the session.

Hard contracting might include reflection in integration stages, review of sessions, addressing session progress and this re-contracting is all recorded in client notes.

Being clear, contracting and re-contracting around therapeutic or learning goals and the focus for the work together is an important part of all EAP and EAL. This is particularly important in EAP sessions which may appear to be a more unstructured, psychotherapy process (compared to more structured EAL psycho-educational program where the client may have purchased a 7-session program).

Let's journey together through the twists and turns of the unique case scenarios and case studies presented in each chapter, whilst reflecting on AWARE Therapy™, and, the wonderful world of EPI practice with horses.

"Horse contact is authentic - what they feel, they express. This is both great modeling for humans, and an opportunity for feedback without judgement."

MEG KIRBY

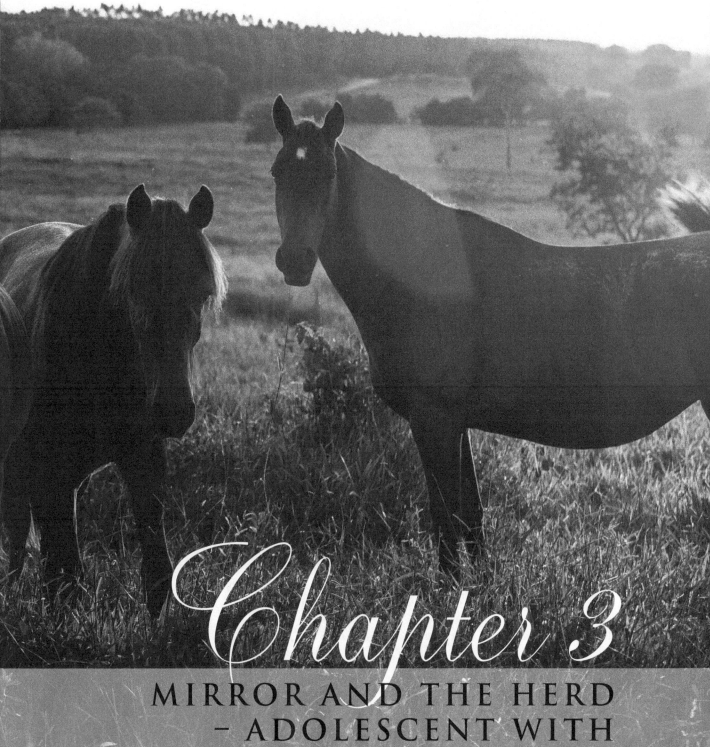

Chapter 3
MIRROR AND THE HERD – ADOLESCENT WITH ANOREXIA

PRACTITIONER
INFORMATION

Dr Anna Cohen is an experienced clinical psychologist who has practiced room-based psychology for 25 years and trained in EAP with the Institute in 2015. Her passion for alternative and effective treatment modalities for children and young people who struggle to engage in formal room-based treatment and for those that find room-based work too confronting and challenging, led to the formation of the 'Heads & Tails' approach. This treatment modality has been Anna's primary focus for the last 5 years.

'Heads & Tails' differs from traditional room-based work as it uses the client's experience in the moment to engage them in therapeutic work. In traditional room-based therapy models, the therapist reflects to the client their feelings and helps to reframe their experience to guide the session. In contrast, 'Heads & Tails' sessions utilise a bottom up process of learning through doing and challenging thoughts through experience, allowing child and adolescent clients to understand how their body language and emotional state affect their interactions and relationships with others. Therefore, in order to connect with the clinical team and horse, clients must learn to self-regulate, manage their emotions, and alter their behaviours.

The 'Heads & Tails' approach is a specialised equine assisted clinical psychology program being offered at Kids & Co. Clinical Psychology, for children and adolescents aged between 5 and 25 years of age with a wide variety of clinical diagnoses and complex needs. It is located in the greater Blue Mountain ranges in NSW, Australia.

CLIENT INFORMATION

PLEASE NOTE: *Charlotte is a pseudonym for the client*

Charlotte, an 18-year-old client, had a long-standing history of Anorexia Nervosa, Anxiety and Self-harming. She initially presented to Kids & Co. aged 14 after a hospital admission in which she was discharged due to "failure to comply with the program".

She presented as extremely underweight, medically unwell (heart, throat, and circulation problems as a consequence of the Anorexia), with depressed and anxious mood and spoke of being traumatised by her admission.

From the age of 14 to 16 Charlotte engaged in intensive Maudsley based family therapy as well as individual therapy. Over this two-year period, she gained weight and all symptomatology abated. She remained in intermittent contact and continued to attend sessions on a monthly basis. She successfully completed her Year 12 obtaining a mark that easily allowed her to gain entry to University for her chosen career.

However, once university commenced in March, she became overwhelmed and again described feelings of low mood, anxiety and a return of her anorexic thinking. As a consequence, she deferred from university and requested regular sessions again occur.

"This is an unfortunate reality for many young clients discharged for non-compliance from traditional, clinical services. Many of these services are not necessarily geared to appeal to and really engage young people in their psychological and therapy treatment."

"Sad, but not uncommon that she was traumatised by her experience in hospital. Many clients can report re-traumatisation after treatment or discharge from clinical inpatient units.

Arguably it is the psychiatric or mental health fields' responsibility to design and offer treatment that is supportive and engaging for young people. EAP is arguably one type of treatment that can foster engagement and results."

"Lucky for Charlotte, the Heads & Tails treatment option was available in their region or area and accessible to her and her family."

REFERRAL/PREPARATION

Heads & Tails sessions were suggested due to the belief that the horses could offer Charlotte a different growth and learning opportunity. Specifically, by offering Charlotte safe equine relationship experiences, whole body experiencing with an emphasis on sensory, somatic and integrated relational learning, self-awareness opportunities, and regulation could be supported. Charlotte had no prior horse experience.

"Many clinicians, clients and parents believe that effective treatment needs to include appropriate sensory, somatic and relationship-focused interventions, alongside traditional cognitive-behavioural interventions. EAP provides this 'whole client', phenomenological, relationship-focused and trauma-informed treatment option."

THE THERAPY GOALS INCLUDED:

• Working with Charlotte's developmental trajectory (including exploring and treating presenting fixed creative adjustments, emerging themes, introjects and contact styles that are impacting on her functioning and wellbeing).

• Focusing on integrating a trauma-informed lens building self-functions and stage 1 trauma skills (around working with strengthening, resourcing, regulating and soothing Charlotte's nervous system, stress response, and developing brain functioning, within her window of tolerance).

• Developing a safe therapeutic alliance with the practitioners in the I-Thou relational container to safely express feelings, needs, build healthy relationship skills and new relational template of emotional safety.

• Practicing within the container of safe, relationship-focused equine experiments that explore Charlotte's emotional, cognitive, behavioural patterns in the here and now (that both support and challenge her within her window of tolerance).

• Developing her awareness and mindfulness skills to support resilience and regulation (sensory, somatic, emotional, cognitive and behavioural awareness).

• An overall reduction of anxiety, low mood and anorexic cognitive patterns.

Heads & Tails is a team-based approach. In each session, there is the the herd of 15 miniature horses, a Clinical Psychologist who is an EAP and an EAP/EAL who work together and alongside the horses as co-facilitators. Miniature horses were selected as they have the same nature as full-sized horses, but we believe that they are less intimidating for work with children and adolescents.

"Therapy Goals included exploring the clients' fixed creative adjustments, which essentially means exploring the early relational field (attachment and care-giving system Charlotte experienced as an infant and child), and specifically how the child 'adjusted' to the early relational field by developing fixed, unconscious patterns in her core beliefs about self, other, the world (her introjects) and in her relationship and behaviour patterns used to regulate and modulate emotion, contact and regulation (her contact styles). These introject-contact style systems underlie and drive presenting behaviour."

"Therapy Goals included regulating the client's nervous system, addressing stress response and brain functioning, so that as Dr Bruce Perry recommends, there was an appropriate bottom up processing treatment approach— working from the brain stem, to the limbic region, to the frontal cortex (cognitive processing and mentalising skills) last."

"Working with awareness over time increases the clients' affect tolerance and overall resilience, as they become less frightened of their experience, body sensations and feelings, and more able to choice-fully express their feelings and needs in non-harming and respectful ways."

"Miniature horses are known to be more like horses, rather than like ponies in their temperament and behaviour. The Heads & Tails team wanted to maximise client safety and effectiveness, hence choosing smaller horses (miniature horses) with the same range of sensitivity and equine behaviours as horses, but smaller bodies and responses, to minimise any risk associated with incidents with potential for physical harm."

The horses are at liberty in their paddock and are free to move in to interact with a client or chose to move away. When an activity is undertaken with a client which requires the horses to be moved out of the herd into another space, the clinical team carefully selects which horse/s will partake in a session to support the therapeutic goals of the client.

Heads & Tails is situated on a large property in the greater Blue Mountains. There are a variety of spaces, such as paddocks, arenas, sheds, stables, a therapy room and round yards, which can be utilised in session the clinical needs of the client. Sessions can be contained to one space or shifted between spaces. For Charlotte's session the arena was selected because of the contained space that it provided.

"Equine experiences with horses at liberty arguably gives the horses increased control over their consent, communications and engagement in the EAP sessions, mimicking real relationship with human-human, who can change, end or leave a relational encounter with another person by ending a conversation, hanging up the phone, leaving a situation, and expressing needs and wants more fully."

"Selection of the horses and therapeutic arena to conduct each EAP session – paddock, stall, stable or arena - are an important part of the ongoing assessment process for practitioners regarding the client's therapeutic goals and unique needs. This requires a solid foundation in equine knowledge of horses in general, knowledge of each herd member, and horse-person-ship skills related to selecting horses and moving horses in and out of client, public and private property spaces."

THE SESSION

CHECK-IN/ASSESSMENT/ CONTRACTING

There was no formal assessment at the Heads & Tails paddock as Charlotte was well known to the EAP team and the team were aware of her. As Charlotte had attended numerous room-based session previously, the check-in was brief as the goals of anxiety and self-harm reduction had already been established in previous sessions.

At the beginning of the session, Charlotte was met in the carpark by the practitioners and walked down into the space. During this time, the team engaged in small talk with Charlotte, such as asking about the trip from Sydney to Heads & Tails, as a means of engaging, building rapport, and settling her into the space.

A check-in with Charlotte was then conducted, specifically regarding how she had been since the previous session, and if there is anything that she wished to specifically do in this session.

This check-in provided the clinical team with an opportunity to understand and observe where Charlotte was emotionally, her words, behaviour (body language, face, posture breath, tension, congruency) and feelings, her contact style, behaviour in here and now, and energy. This enabled us to meet her there. Charlotte stated being excited to experience a Heads & Tails session and was visibly keen to move into the paddock and meet the herd.

"This here and now assessment enables the practitioner to track current presentation, that may be different to historic presentation and be present to client."

INITIAL EQUINE EXPERIENCE

As Charlotte moved out into the herd, the horses were calm and settled. She invited 3 of the horses (Mirror, Coco and Soda) to join her session in the arena.

In the arena, Charlotte was asked to make a river with bends (using different objects such as sticks, balls, and pool noodles) to represent challenges and obstacles in her life.

As Charlotte worked, the horses outside the arena were very quiet and still, behaviour which is unusual for them. The three horses in the arena with Charlotte focused on one section of the river, and they persistently moved it (the river) wider, and intently mouthed and pawed at the objects.

As Charlotte continued to place objects at this bend, all three horses focused their attention on removing anything she placed here. Charlotte commented, "They are not happy about this...they are uncomfortable." She then silently and mindfully focused on patting and reassuring the horses. With this, two horses moved away.

Charlotte, together with our horse Mirror, spent a significant amount of time at this bend and silently negotiated the space. As Charlotte worked on the river, she reflected to the team how the horses seemed

"The practitioner asked the client to choose herd members for her activity, out of a larger herd, and she chose 3 horses. It would be interesting to hear some more about how she made this decision, and what she felt about these horses in particular. This would enable the client to express her feelings, thoughts, needs, projection, and perspective through the process of selecting horses."

"Projective experiments can be an effective way to support self-exploration with degrees of externalisation, natural titration, movement of whole-self in the experience and creative process. This can help some clients tap into their own wisdom, that is not connected to logical thinking or cognitive process, but more somatic, emotional and relational wisdom that can unfold in being in the here and now and responding/adapting to current experience."

"The client is making her own meaning of the horses' behaviour and choices, and how this may apply to her. She is expressing agency, will, and meaning-making."

"Really uncomfortable...they don't really like this part (the bend)."

Charlotte further reflected how the horses seemed 'stuck' at this section. As she reflected to the team, Mirror moved in towards Charlotte, and was observed to wrap his head around her waist and support her.

"Stuck is the word that emerges for Charlotte, this sounds important for her, and her life currently."

PROCESSING AND DEEPENING

Charlotte decided to remove the bend, and with this, all horses in the arena again became settled and still. Charlotte was present to this change and commented, "They are happy now."

At this point, the team stated to Charlotte, "Notice what that feels like inside." Charlotte sat with this silently, and as she did, Mirror faced her and was intent on muzzling her. With this, Charlotte kept saying to the team, "He is happy now."

"Here, the role of the horse/s (as change agent) changes, from 'unique feedback' and projection (expanding her metaphor dialogue and meaning-making), to offering Charlotte a relational experience of 'Confirmation' – where the client feels deeply seen and valued by the other (horse)."

Charlotte was asked by team to take Mirror through the river. Charlotte successfully led Mirror to the end of the river at the arena fence. As she tried to turn him around and walk him back through the river, Mirror was immovable.

"Another equine experiment is offered after the initial projective experiment. The leading experiment appears to increase the relational exchange between client and horse."

At this, Charlotte reflected to the team, "There is no point going back." She took a long pause, and sadness overcame her. The team reflected that going forward was blocked. As this was said, the colour drained from Charlotte's face, and her whole body looked helpless. Dr Cohen then asked, "What do we need to do to go forward?" Charlotte shared, "I need to make a change before I can move forward again."

"Client's emergent themes include deepening into her feeling of sadness, and of stuckness."

"Practitioner inquiry oriented the client to what is needed here? And the client offers that she needs to make a change. With this insight, sadness and tears arrive again. The insight and feelings support her to remove the block and open out her river, to move into mobilisation, action and contact with what most matters to her."

With this, Mirror then left, and Charlotte became teary. Charlotte removed the block and opened out her river. The team then suggested to Charlotte that she walk through the river again and asked if she would like to take Mirror with her. Charlotte's affect changed, and she purposefully moved to Mirror. He however, was not wanting to move.

The team asked if she would like them (the practitioner team) to join her and she nodded. Together the team and Charlotte walked through the river, and Mirror spontaneously followed. After a walk through the river together, Charlotte wanted to continue walking through it, but did so without the team. As she walked through the river several times, Mirror started to shift away. Charlotte reflected, "He knows I can do it alone now."

To further deepen her experience, Charlotte was asked if she would like to spend some time in her river. Charlotte stated, "I will sit here for a while and then I will move out from here." As she silently sat, the three horses stood facing away from her and were very still. After several minutes, Charlotte picked up her seat and, with purpose, left the space with a beaming smile and approached the clinicians.

The team asked what she thought Mirror's behaviour reflected, she stated, "He knows I can do it now." The team reflected, "Yes, he does. He knows you can do it." Charlotte added, "rather, he knows Charlotte can do it." "I am doing it!" The team asked what that was like for her, she replied, "It feels good."

"This practitioner offer was to check in with whether the client needed more support or would like to negotiate the next part of the life-challenge alone, she opted for support. The therapeutic alliance illicited some independence, with Charlotte wanting to complete the walk without the team."

"The team can see, and Mirror knows "I can do it alone now." Signalling a move towards self-trust and agency."

"I love this offer for deepening and integration, allowing the client to be with herself, her feelings, her knowing and decisions."

"This is an important indicator that the client has arrived at her own knowing, that she believes "he knows" (the horse, and potentially others witnessing know now too). The final statement of "I can do it" is a signal that integration has occurred, the client has digested the process and feels a sense of internal certainty and ownership… in gestalt terms the 'figure of interest' has moved through the cycle of experience from awareness, to action, to contact, to integration and closure!"

INTEGRATION & CLOSURE

Charlotte was asked by the team what she would like to do with her construction. She replied, "I will pack it away. I don't need it anymore." As this was said, Soda lay down with her back to the two clinicians and Charlotte. Charlotte was able to approach and touch Soda, from behind the horse's line of vision, without Soda so much as moving her ear. All three horses were completely still, as were the other four horses outside the arena. The sound of the trees moving gently in the breeze and the distant sounds of the chickens and other horses was all that could be heard.

"The horses, other animals and natural environment all contributed to this quiet moment in a beautiful example of the Wisdom Approach in action."

43

The session ended with Charlotte being asked if she would be open to spending 30-45 minutes of her car ride thinking about the process and reflecting on this. She was also asked to write a reflection if she wanted to. The suggestion of writing a reflection was the practitioners' recommendation, in the hope that the client may tap into further resourcing, deepening and integration of the work.

"This is a homework piece that can be supportive for some clients in the integration and closure stages of the session. This was thought to be a further support for deepening and integration of the session due to the knowledge that this client regularly liked to reflect on her sessions. Some clients respond well to this, others do not!"

REFLECTION

Charlotte did the majority of this hour-long exercise in silence and/or without engaging the clinical team. The only moments of dialogue were those narrated. As she left, she said the experience was "profoundly powerful" and hugged her mother stating, "This was so worth it." Her mother commented, "Horsey time is such fun." To which Charlotte emphatically replied, "Mum this was way more than horse time. This was profound."

As a very seasoned clinician, it takes a lot to really move me, however, I was holding back tears. Profound is truly what this experience was for both the EAL that was working with Charlotte and myself.

"Often times we think therapy should involve a lot more talking to be effective, but this session involved minimal dialogue, and yet appeared to be very engaging and meaningful for the client."

"It is a special opportunity for practitioners to hear the clients themselves self-report that the session has in fact been profound for them!"

"It is so important for practitioners to be real, to be present, moved, and choicefully bracketing and containing feelings, in the service of the clients' needs. Sometimes, it is useful to self-disclose and share. In this moment, with this client it was enough to be aware of the experience of feeling moved, deeply connected to the client and session, but to contain it to support the client to have their own powerful experience, meaning-making and process."

" *We become who we are by learning to be where we are – with acceptance, kindness and open curiosity.* "

MEG KIRBY

Chapter 4
SPACE AND SHANI - 6 YEAR OLD BOY WITH AUTISM

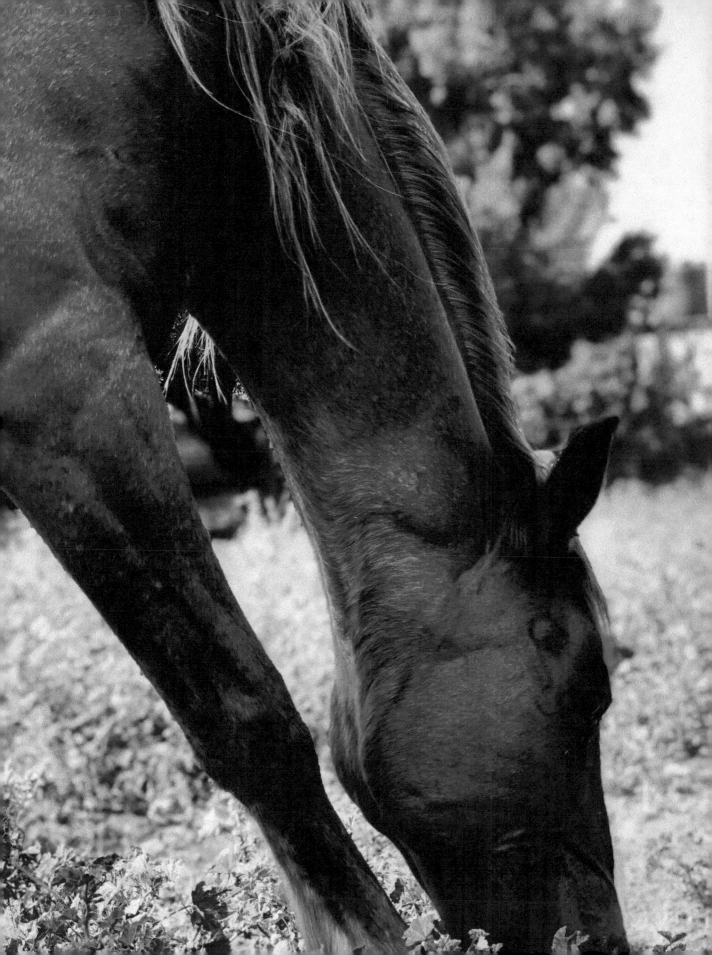

PRACTITIONER INFORMATION

ANN POULSEN is an experienced Steiner Education Teacher and registered Counsellor practicing in the wider Bryon Bay region of Australia. Ann trained with the Equine Psychotherapy Institute in 2014 and has a special interest in qualitative research, science, children, and horses. Ann practices equine assisted psychotherapy and equine assisted learning from her stunning home property, Burringbar Equine Centre.

CLIENT INFORMATION

PLEASE NOTE: *Jasper is a pseudonym for the client*

Jasper booked in for an Equine Assisted Learning (EAL) session after a recommendation from a local therapist. Jasper is a high functioning 6-year-old on the autism spectrum. He lives at home with his parents as a single child.

Initial phone information with mother clarified that Jasper had been given a number of diagnoses, including Autism Spectrum Disorder, Attention Deficit Hyperactivity Disorder (ADHD), Oppositional Defiance Disorder (ODD), as well as auditory processing issues, a speech disorder, and high anxiety.

He also had severe allergic reactions to certain substances and was currently on medication for ADHD. He had previously attended speech therapy, occupational therapy, and learning support sessions.

Jasper's mother, Andrea, explained over the phone that Jasper was having difficulties at school and at home. He was becoming increasingly anti-social and isolated from the other children in his class. In the classroom, his disruptive behaviour included hitting, biting, and refusing to cooperate. This had resulted in poor relationships with his teacher and classmates. He was now only attending half days and was regularly resistant to going to school at all. At home he was having difficulty following instructions, having anger outbursts, throwing things and being unkind to the family dog.

"Sadly, many young children on the autism spectrum can present with other behavioural and social difficulties that escalate until the child receives good support and interventions."

Jaspers mum hoped the EAL experiences would help him to calm down and have more self-control. I explained that the sessions could offer Jasper an opportunity to connect with the horses and offer an opportunity for him to (potentially) learn about relationships. In this way, over time, the horses could become a resource for Jasper and support him to recognise, monitor and begin to regulate his emotions and emotional outbursts. This is what we hoped for.

"A resource is any activity that supports a sense of safety and somatic, emotional and cognitive wellbeing."

"Once children learn to name the horses' feelings, and their feelings, safely express their feelings (and watch the horses' express their feelings) they can begin to develop affective regulation skills."

Together with mother Andrea we identified some specific learning goals for Jasper to:

• Become more self-aware and interested in the "other"

• Recognise what "others" like and do not like

• Learn to follow instructions – listening and following through

• Develop the capacity to calm himself, to regulate himself

• Have improved capacity to regulate his emotions (including expressing his feelings in non-harming ways)

• Build resilience and self-confidence

These were big learning goals but I was hopeful with regular weekly sessions we could support Jasper to work towards these in a positive, fun learning environment.

When Andrea asked what she should tell him about our sessions, I asked her to simply tell him he was coming out to visit the horses. No need for any lengthy explanations. I wanted him to feel as relaxed and comfortable as possible when he arrived at this new environment for the first time. I planned on bringing two of the horses into a safe grassy area, where they were free to move around.

SESSION PREPARATION

It was important to me for Jasper to feel safe during our session together. During our initial check-in, I planned to invoke the least amount of fear possible while carefully offering the safety guideline and speaking with him about the nature of horses and how they might behave.

I prepared myself before the session by breathing, grounding and noticing how I was feeling both physically and emotionally. I knew this process, the 4 Steps to Awareness, would also support Jasper to be more aware while he was with me.

"The EPI Model, which teaches the 4 Steps to Awareness, ensures that all EAP/ EAL practitioners are present, grounded and self-aware prior to and during sessions, to ensure client-focused sessions and client psychological safety. This is seen as an essential competency for effective and professional facilitation."

51

My developmental belief is that the first 7 years children inherently trust the adults around them and look to those adults for security and guidance. Whatever I hold in my consciousness when I work with a child inevitably impacts the direction and outcome of the EAL session we are doing together. Doing the 4 Steps to Awareness before a child arrives carries both of us through the session in as safe, grounded and present space as possible.

FIRST SESSION

As Jasper climbed out of his car seat and walked over to the table and chairs just outside the horse yards, he glanced briefly over at the horses and ran to sit down. I thought this was unusual behaviour. I introduced myself and we chatted briefly about his age, school and if he had seen horses before. We talked a little about horses and I invited him to tell me anything he knew about them. I told a brief story about my horses to illustrate a safety point.

During this time, I was getting a picture of the child and how he might respond in the session and around the horses. I was also observing his physical characteristics, the quality of his voice and speech, his body language, mannerisms and so on. Jasper presented as tall for his age, quite thin with sandy coloured hair, blue eyes, a pale complexion and a melancholic disposition. He spoke slowly but not often.

In my experience over the past 5 years of working with children in an EAL context and over 18 years as a classroom teacher, I generally find myself trying to slow down young children. Not to dampen their enthusiasm but to bring more awareness into their will – their actions and tasks.

In EAL sessions, children are especially enthusiastic to get going but quite often they are unaware of the risks involved with interacting with horses. I usually

"EPI Field theory dictates that humans are always mutually influencing and co-creating each-others' experience in relationship. Hence, practitioners take great care to be intentional about their presence, attitude, language and approach with clients."

"The 4 Steps to Awareness is a trademarked set of mindfulness exercises that I developed in the EPI Model, to support resourcing and awareness for the client. The practitioner utilises it before the session, and often-times, facilitates it directly with clients, depending on the age, stage and trauma history of the client."

"This is an important part of our assessment process, gathering verbal and non-verbal information about the client, assessing for safety and for client themes, needs and presenting issues."

encourage children to do some horse "outbreaths" and some horse "steps" before going out into the paddock with the horses.

However, with Jasper things were very different. I could tell from the start he was unenthusiastic about approaching the horses. Interestingly, Jasper presented to me as a reserved, shy and cautious child, quite the opposite of what I had expected after hearing his mother's description of him and his behaviours at home and at school.

After a while of talking and looking at the horses in the paddock, I asked Jasper if he would like to meet the small black Shetland pony named Shani. He looked apprehensive, so I added, "In a way that feels safe for you."

Very suddenly Jasper jumped up out of his seat and ran to his mother's car shouting, "This is where I feel safe." He quickly shut the car door and locked himself in! Taking a moment to observe this behaviour, I decided to carry on as if nothing out of the ordinary had happened.

In an EAL session, it is always important to try and be with whatever shows up, to observe and support the client to work through their process as much as possible. The car was parked where Jasper had full view of the horse yard from out of the front window. I reassured his mother, letting her know that we would let the situation unfold as calmly and gently as possible.

As I went into the paddock to greet Shani and start to pat her, I noticed Jasper's face looking up over the car seat watching us. He watched for a while as I stroked and groomed the pony until his curiosity overcame his fear and he opened up the car door and slowly emerged.

He walked from the car and came to the gate. I asked him if he was ready to say hello to Shani. He nodded and came through the gate holding my hand

"In assessment, it is so important to gather history and referral information, but, to rely heavily on the phenomenological data, the here and now assessment information that is emerging with the client, rather than on what is said, documented or previously reported about the client."

"This is an important moment where the practitioner supported Jasper to orient around safety, awareness and choice, and to do what made him feel safe."

"This is a good example of phenomenological practice, staying with the pacing, emerging themes and behaviours of the client. This is very different to a solution focused approach, where the agenda dictates the practitioners' responses to request or require the client to behave or respond in a certain way. "

"What a delightful moment here! Jasper was given the space and time, and the locus of control to orient around his own safety needs. To watch and experience from a safe distance, supporting good trauma-informed practice of what we call titration (a drop at a time of activating or disturbance of the homeostasis), supporting the client to stay inside their window of tolerance, (if they were outside their window of tolerance, the client is at risk of flooding, overwhelm or re-traumatisation). He approached when he was ready. One of Dr Bruce Perry's trauma informed and tentatively stepping toward her. We stopped after each step, just to look and notice. We didn't speak, but I could tell his curiosity and interest were leading him towards her.

Finally, Jasper was able to approach and touch Shani lightly on the neck. He noticed how soft she was and how her skin twitched at his touch on her wither. He rapidly lost himself in a sensory experience with the pony as he picked up every brush I had and tried each one out on her.

This touching experience calmed Jasper down, his voice became quieter and his movements less agitated. Jasper had noticeably relaxed and his growing curiosity encouraged him to explore different ways of touching and brushing Shani.

We noticed together how she responded to the different brushes and he told me which ones she liked the best and how he knew. We noticed the tiniest shiver of her skin at the lightest touch in a sensitive place, the way her tail swished lightly, then rapidly, back and forth. We noticed together how her ears turned to listen to our voices.

These observations, and this communication between the three of us, was a significant beginning to Jaspers EAL journey. We thanked Shani for letting us touch her and brush her and reluctantly Jasper said goodbye to her. He gave her a big cuddle and ran out to tell his mum all about her.

I asked Jasper if he would like to see Shani again and he said yes confidently. I suggested his mum and I speak on the phone in a few days' time. There was no need to ask Jasper too many questions as it was very clear from his behaviour how he was impacted. I suggested he might like to do a drawing of Shani and show it to me next time. Children are often overwhelmed by questions and analytical discussions. I felt Jasper needed to "soak" in his experience with the pony for as long as possible.

"principles is always to ensure the child has choice to participate in therapeutic experiences."

"Interventions that focus on outer zone awareness, touch, sensory experiences in a safe relational container is what supports regulation, resourcing, and over-time with repetition, ultimately healing for many trauma clients."

"Notice how this touching experiment and therapeutic process appears so simple (and can have such an impact physically and emotionally on clients), however, this facilitation actually requires a lot of skill in the practitioner, resulting in the client being regulated, and his natural orienting and social engagement system coming back on line."

"A lot of 'other awareness', listening, tracking and being in relationship skills being developed here, in the safe therapeutic alliance."

"What an important transition from the beginning of the session, to the end of the session – supported by client-focused practice, phenomenological and trauma-informed practice."

"This is an important part of child-sensitive work - more observation and relationship focus, and less inquiry and self-awareness inquiry."

As I reflected on the session, I was pleased to have made the choice to leave Jasper in the car until he was ready to come out. I knew Jasper was doing the best he could at the time and I trusted in the process we had begun. This allowed me to be really present with what was going on and it gave Jasper the time he needed to regulate the intense feelings he was having, in a place where he felt safe. He was then able to go beyond his initial fear and explore the unfamiliar. Being present with whatever arises is one of the essential "skills and practices" required from an EAL Practitioner.

Later over the phone, Andrea and I agreed Jasper had come a long way in the session. He had moved through his anxiety and fear around being in different surroundings, to experiencing pleasure and joy with the pony. She expressed her delight that he had talked about Shani for days and had told his teacher and class-mates about his experience. We booked sessions for Jasper at regular weekly times.

FOLLOWING SESSIONS

Jasper arrived for his second EAL session with great enthusiasm. He spotted Shani as soon as he got out of the car and was ready and eager to get started. Such a change from our first meeting!

I asked Jasper what he had remembered from last time about the horses. He told me that Shani had liked being brushed and especially liked being patted on the tummy. It was wonderful to feel how much our connection had developed in just one session together.

After our brief check-in, Jasper took my hand and invited me to go into the yard with him to greet Shani. Together we noticed where she was standing and how she greeted us. This gave me an opportunity to introduce Jasper to the idea of a personal space boundaries and what that might look like for the pony and how she might let us know when we touched into her boundaries.

"Integration happens in a different way for children compared to adults, and it is important to practice with child-appropriate skills. The 'homework' integration offer was also a developmentally appropriate invitation."

"Vital practice of trusting the process and what comes up in each moment, and tracking closely the client's readiness, emerging needs and themes and window of tolerance."

"Again, this is a significant shift in the clients' behaviour and capacity from Session 1 to Session 2."

"What a lovely opportunity for client determination, locus of control, confidence and choice. Safe relationship and the previous session experience, supported the client to make such important personal shift from anxiety and fear to regulation, confidence, open curiosity and initiating."

"Boundary practice is integral in the EPI Model, the horse wisdom program, and trauma-informed practice."

55

In this way, I was beginning to have a conversation with Jasper about personal space boundaries. We decided together when Shani was saying yes to being approached and when she was saying no. Jasper told me why he thought she might be saying no at times. He said sometimes he said no as well. We talked a little about the times when we say yes and sometimes when we say no, and how both are necessary.

We discussed times when saying yes or no, might not be the right choice. For example, saying no to your teacher might not be ok, if he is asking you to stay away from something dangerous (i.e. a hot stove top).

As our sessions together continued, Jasper developed a wonderful friendship with the small black pony and the other horses. He loved to take Shani out for walks. At times when he was particularly rough or bossy, the pony would let him know with a shove of her rump or laid-back ears. He was quick to respond to these signals from the pony and understood she did not like his rough behaviour.

Jasper really enjoyed his developing friendship with Shani and his mother confided to me that the pony was becoming an important resource for Jasper. He would often refer to her, how she might respond in certain situations, or how she would be there waiting when he arrived to see her.

We had certainly begun to address our learning goals very early on in our time together and over the course of the next few months we observed some remarkable changes in Jasper. He had so much more self-confidence, not just around the ponies but also at home and at school.

After his sessions with the horses Jasper was noticeably calmer and over time his anxiety lessened and his emotional outbursts became less frequent. He understood other children could be hurt by unkind actions and words and he became more caring toward others. Jasper became more willing to follow directions and to respect other peoples' boundaries.

"This is a nice example of how the client is learning in a 'live relationship' about foundation relationship skills including being aware of others' feelings, needs, boundaries, and adapting one's behaviour according to the needs and wants of the other. The bio-feedback of the horses give clients an opportunity to develop awareness skills, relationship skills and learning to creatively adjust (instead of being stuck in old, out of date, unconscious and fixed patterns of thinking, believing and behaving)."

"This is an example of how EAP sessions can over time support a transitioning from learning with the horses and within the EAP session to generalise out to other domains of life, at home, at school and improving the child's mental state, mental health in general and behaviour. Important to note is the development of relationship and empathy skills are very often a natural accompaniment of EAP (and so vital for many children, presenting with psychiatric diagnoses)."

It was truly a heart-warming experience to observe Jasper's learning with the horses, especially Shani. We continued to work together over the next 12 months and Jasper grew in confidence, resilience and understanding. I'm so grateful for the amazing support given by the horses and for the opportunity be a part of the beautiful children's healing and development journeys.

"This is what many EAP and EAL practitioners report, a real gratitude for what the horses, the EPI Model and how being with clients in this way can be ultimately resourcing and growth-full for the practitioners' themselves. A wonderful part, or benefit, of this work is enrichment for all parties - for client, horse and practitioner!"

Chapter 5

HERD AND COUNTRY - INDIGENOUS CHILD AND FAMILY SESSION

PRACTITIONER INFORMATION

SARAH E. FERGUSON is an experienced Counsellor, Therapist and Support Worker at The Gatepost Support Services in Gunnedah in the rural North West NSW region. A current Level 4 member of The Australia Counselling Association, Sarah brought to her EPI EAP training a Masters in Narrative Therapy and Community Work, a Bachelor of Counselling, Certification in Hypnotherapy and Neuro-linguistic Programming and forty five years' experience of being in relationships with horses. In 2020, Sarah began a PhD with the University of Queensland investigating the welfare and ethical considerations of horses in Equine Assisted Psychotherapy,

Passionate about rural living, horses, rural therapy and research, Sarah brings a down to earth direct integrity to her work, which supports her to work well with Indigenous clients and community, male clients, school groups and management in her EAP and EAL services.

CLIENT BACKGROUND INFORMATION

PLEASE NOTE: *Zachariah is a pseudonym for the client*

Zachariah had already been a participant in our adapted eight session EPI Horse Wisdom Program® delivered for a local primary school. During Horse Wisdom, Zachariah was almost mute. I was contacted by Family and Community Services (FACS) and requested to provide six sessions of individual Equine Assisted Psychotherapy.

There were three no shows (non-attendance), then Zachariah showed up for a session with his dad, Jimmy.

Within the Horse Wisdom program delivered at school, the individual therapeutic goal (separate from the group) for Zachariah included relationship development and finding safe space for expression.

My observation during the school-based Horse Wisdom Program® was that Zachariah was in a retroflective pattern – suppressing expression. His tendency was to completely shut down, unable to speak at all. I wondered about whether there was a disowned part of anger or aggression on the other end of the spectrum. This information informed, but did not drive, the individual session. I try to stay out of the way of what I think is going on, to let what IS going on arrive in the space.

FIRST SESSION

FATHER AND SON (PARENT-CHILD SESSION)

Jimmy and Zachariah arrive together.

Jimmy is the father of seven children, with a history of being in and out of gaol and struggling with addiction to drugs and alcohol. The children had been

"A Retroflection pattern is a contact style (behavioural pattern) that commonly presents as the client holding in or holding back expressing what they think, feel, want and, commonly, presenting somatically as a "blunted or flat affect" – mental state examination terminology which refers to when affect is constricted, the range and intensity of expression are reduced. In blunted affect, emotional expression is further reduced. To diagnose flat affect, virtually no signs of affective expression are present; the client's voice may be monotone and the face may be immobile. Depression and mutism can be an extreme form of retroflection."

"This is a good example of EPI Model phenomenological practice, gathering assessment information, and staying open to what is happening in the here and now for the client, rather than historic assessment, assumption and meaning. This way, the client, as they present, is most important, leading the way rather than practitioner hypotheses or agenda leading the way, ensuring a client-centred and experiential approach rather than a practitioner-centred, cognitive approach."

removed from Jimmy's care several times in the past due to Jimmy being drug and alcohol affected. At this time, the children were back with Jimmy and mother, but the children remained under the shared care of FACS (Family and Community Services) indefinitely.

I offered for both Jimmy and Zachariah to engage in some breathing, grounding and outer zone orienting through the senses. I then introduced the safety guideline followed by an invitation for them to meet the horses at liberty and a touch and groom experiment.

The focus for the equine experience was on noticing what the horses were expressing with their bodies, and what the horses liked and didn't like in their contact and approach with father and son.

It went very well. Both were comfortable with silence. The phenomenological inquiry focused on the here and now experience of being with the horses and there was no deepening into emerging themes, as it felt too soon for that.

Jimmy (father) spoke a fair bit about what he'd noticed and how he knew what it meant. I observed Jimmy becoming task oriented and interacting silently with Zachariah, offering him brushes, putting his hand over Zachariah's, and showing him long slow strokes for grooming one of the horse's belly. The silence seemed serene and easy. Zachariah's smile spoke the words he couldn't say. Both were looking forward to next session.

SECOND SESSION

FATHER, SON & SIBLINGS (UNPLANNED FAMILY SESSION)

Two weeks later, I was expecting just Zachariah and his Dad for our second session. The taxi arrived and delivered both, as well as fourteen -year-old Jackson and eight-year-old Grady.

"This is a typical EPI Model format that includes awareness practices, trauma-informed practices, open experiment to build a relationship with the herd members, with a safety briefing. This kind of sequence and experiment has wide applications clinically, and is a great way to allow emerging themes and behaviours to be assessed and to orient treatment or therapy to both a skill building and psychotherapeutic trajectory."

"Focus on others' (the horses) feelings, behaviours, needs and boundaries are essential relationship skills and being inherently relational, offer a window into the clients' internalised relationship model and projections."

"This is a wonderful example of the richness of this experiential form of therapy. EAP offers a relationship focus, in a meaningful and real way. The father and son experienced being together, perhaps in a way that met some of the boy's unmet needs for attunement and mirroring. There was joy, space, relationship and what we call in gestalt therapy contact – the lifeblood of growth and healing."

I was at a choice-point. I could have had Jackson and Grady excluded and asked them to wait inside and continued with the planned session. However, I didn't do that because Zachariah introduced them. He spoke to me! I recognised that I had an opportunity that could be useful for the whole family. Tricky choice. Who is the client? I need to remember that Zachariah was still the client. I had to hold that clearly in my mind.

I immediately created some observing, assessing and planning space by taking some time fetching waivers for Jackson and Grady, and having Jimmy sign them. During that time, I was paying a great deal of attention to the interactions between the four of them to try to get an idea of the dynamics.

I had a moment during the form filling when I had to bracket my own response, which I am familiar with and know well. The waiver requires birthdates, and I always frame that question with "Do you know what date you were born?" so there isn't an assumption that they should know, and less likelihood of shame if they don't know their birth date. Nobody in the family knew their birthdate. Jimmy said he couldn't remember as there were too many kids. I said it didn't matter anyway.

Jackson had his head down on the desk during most of this five-minute exercise. Grady was chattering and has a speech impediment that sometimes made it hard to comprehend him. He was trying to tell me what Zachariah had told him about coming out. I casually asked Zachariah if there was anything else he'd shared, and he spoke! He said he'd told Grady about the horses as herd, prey, play animals and about breathing into your feet. To be honest, I had to hide my surprise. Jackson looked up and said, "He told me too." "The same stuff, or different stuff?" I asked. "He talked about Ollie. He likes Ollie," Jackson said and then he put his head back on the desk.

"The choice point was informed by many things, but particularly by Zachariah moving from a previously mute presentation into talking and introducing his family! What a clinical change. The practitioner often has to respond fast, adapt and orient to what is happening – these creative, adaptive and experimenting skills of the EPI practitioner is what really separates this model from other EAP/ EAL models, the theory and practice methodology requires practitioners to build these gestalt therapy skills, and utilise in the service of the clients' needs."

"I like the transparency here, as often there are moments when we as practitioners can utilise to make fast assessments, reflect, orient and then use that information to design an appropriate equine experiment, tailored to suit the entire family! The waivers are a legal and ethical requirement, and, offered reflection and time for the practitioner to assess and formulate an appropriate family experiment. Working with experiments is a big part of gestalt therapy, and EPI Model of EAP. Experiments support brain, body and behavioural based learning and therapy interventions. Cognitive therapy is not always appropriate or useful for particular client groups or clients, depending on their trauma history, diagnosis and current functioning. This client family group is a great example of how EAP can offer a more engaging and appropriate client-sensitive, experiential, brain-behavioural based intervention, than a room based, cognitive based intervention/approach."

"Bracketing is one of the phenomenological skills that EPI Practitioners develop during training, and is a core competency for EAP and EAL practitioners. The practitioner's beliefs and politics do not belong in the session, and need to be brought to personal therapy and reflection and/or supervision. The practitioner successfully bracketed her own response, allowing her to stay in the session with Zachariah's and the family's emerging needs and themes."

"Zachariah was impacted by the session and shared with family members specific details. Important skills and development for the practitioner to notice and track."

Another choice-point arrived for me. Do I directly address Jackson, with further inquiry and engagement, or work around his edges, and keep track of it internally in my mind, but not follow through into verbal inquiry? I decided to approach Jackson less directly and keep assessing him.

Jimmy was fidgety and I was beginning to suspect he was stoned. Choice-point was whether I involve him, but safely, or ask him to sit it out. I decided to involve him safely.

Grady and Zachariah seemed attentive. I quickly decided on a plan for the following fifty minutes, as the taxi would be arriving to pick them up, leaving little room for unstructured or casual time management.

The therapeutic plan needed to involve minimal talking and an invitation to Jackson to join in if he wanted or sit out if he didn't. The focus of the session revolved around the emergent theme of noticing expression.

I then proceeded to offer some introductory awareness and trauma-informed practices (inviting Zachariah to assist if he wanted), offered the safety briefing (in relation to interacting with the horses, including information about the nature and be-haviour of horses) and then offered an experiment to *meet the herd of four horses, noticing who you are drawn to and make contact.*

I gave a bucket of brushes, offering an opportunity to groom if they wished, noticing the horses' com-munications, specifically *what the horses are telling you about what they like and don't like and whether it is loud and clear or quiet and difficult to read.*

I decided to ask Jimmy (father) to stay outside the paddock, to ensure safety, but to still be engaged by *watching what the horses are doing with their bodies and how they express their feelings.*

"The phenomenological inquiry example ("the same stuff or different stuff?") uses client-appropriate words, attuning to the clients' developmental age, stage, functioning and culture."

"There are endless choice-points as EAP practitioners- opportunities to inquire, observe, track, orient and design experiments. It is great to hear about the practitioner's internal process and track her choice-point reflection, whilst in session, as this is a 'behind the scene' learning opportunity for the reader/learner."

"The choice-point (of including Jimmy safely) will depend on relevant contracts, ethical issues, practitioner window of tolerance, client groups, and much more! This is a complex, but important, choice-point. Each practitioner will assess and respond uniquely, depending on their approach and codes of professional conduct and ethics."

"This choice-point ensured the father's and children's safety, and the horses' safety, yet still keep him engaged in the process from a safe vantage point. This avoided a potential shaming of father by having to acknowledge or inquire about whether he was indeed under the influence of drugs, in the presence of his sons."

Approximately thirty-five minutes total for the equine experiences, would keep it within fifty minutes although the plan was not as structured as that!

Zachariah said he wanted me to facilitate the initial awareness and resourcing exercises, so I did. Jackson didn't get up off the seat, but was participating, and so, during one awareness exercise I said, "You might not be able to notice your bum...try and squeeze it tight and see what you can notice." Jackson rose a little in the seat, so I knew he had done it! His head came off the desk for that time too.

I asked Zachariah what awareness is and he said, "Keeps you safe." I added, "It gives you the choice to respond and thrive in life." He said, "Yeah, that too". I asked Zachariah if he wanted to tell the others what boundaries are and he said, "My yes and no." I said maybe the others needed a bit more information and he said something like, "You only do what you want to do and if you don't like it you have to let the horses know."

I expanded on that a bit to include some idea of what that might look like, like walking away or gently moving the horse's head or asking for support to communicate a personal space boundary with the horses.

Another choice-point emerged for me at this time – to keep asking Zachariah (which could strengthen the new knowledge and learning) or facilitate the rest of the safety guideline and warm up exercises myself. I chose to do the rest myself, since time was so precious. I then did the herd, prey, play talk and made the invitation to first experiment at liberty. Again, I said they could come or not, whatever they liked.

The four horses were already in the liberty yard. Ollie, Mabel, Ralph and Ned. We all walked over. Jimmy stayed outside the yard as planned, I asked Jimmy what he was going to be doing, saying something like, "Jeez Jimmy, what was it that I said you could do?" like I was forgetful and he said, "Just

"Interesting that Zachariah had recalled or integrated on some level that being aware can support safety with the horses and in life, and with minimal prompts shared this new knowledge. This is a good sign regarding the effectiveness of the EAP sessions and the capacity to remember, recall and perhaps integrate this new learning."

"Another different kind of choice point – when to support your client to facilitate a part of the session? This can be a wonderful and empowering intervention that can enhance learning opportunities, and support a range of therapeutic goals such as increasing locus of control, increasing initiating and communication skills. Understandably, time was of the essence!"

watching and noticing stuff." I went, "Yeah, that's right, right, great, I'll be doing the same hey.".

I invited them to meet each horse, in whatever way felt safe and right for each of them. I said, "Meet each horse individually and choose a horse you are drawn to and make contact."

Jackson and Zachariah stepped into the yard first. Grady hesitated at the gate. He turned and looked at me and so I simply said, "Whatever feels okay for you." He stood just inside the gate.

Some practitioner observations included:

• Jackson moved all around the yard quite quickly.

• Ralphie and Ollie (horses) stood still and he patted them then quickly moved off.

• Walking quickly to Ned and Mabel (horses) had them both walk away.

• Jackson kept walking around the yard

Zachariah was watching Jackson. He moved slowly and quietly to the side of the yard and just stood there. Ollie (horse) walked over to Zachariah. They stood there together watching Jackson as he kept walking around.

After a while, Zachariah walked over to Ned (horse) and stopped about two metres from him. Ned turned to him, eyes wide open and ears forward. Zachariah held out his hand. At that moment, Mabel (horse) spotted some fencing supplies sitting outside the fence near the top gate and, as Mabel does, went into curiosity mode, head up, tail up, high stepping, weaving back and forward as she inched closer for a look.

Jackson stopped walking and started watching her. Zachariah and Ned (horse) both looked at her. Grady, who had just met Ralph (horse) who walked up to him and was smelling him, didn't notice anything and Ralph (horse) also took no notice of Mabel.

Jimmy (father) nodded at me and then nodded in the direction of the top gate. I understood what he

"The practitioner is ensuring that there is an appropriate 'goodness of fit' between her language and the father's language to increase the likelihood of a strong therapeutic relationship and really meeting the client 'where they are at'."

"Relationship is the therapeutic focus here."

was thinking and nodded back. Jimmy slowly walked around the outside of the yard up towards the fencing equipment. Mabel danced over to the fence that Jimmy was walking up and trotted beside him as he approached the wire. Jimmy leant down and touched the roll of wire, looked up at Mabel, who was now just beside the top gate, took a step towards her and held out his hand. She smelt his hand, gave a snort, turned around and started grazing. Jimmy slowly walked back to where I was. He smiled.

During this time, Zachariah and Ned (horse) had come together – both kept watching. Zachariah's hand was on Ned's neck, just gently stroking him. Ralph (horse) had left Grady and approached Jackson, who had stood still throughout Mabel's (horse) exhibition. Grady had followed Ralph out into the yard and both he and Jackson were patting Ralph. Jackson moved away to where Zachariah was patting Ned (horse). Zachariah moved away and Jackson began patting Ned. Ned's head was bobbing and his eyes were closing. Zachariah moved over to Ollie (horse), who was standing near Jimmy (father) and I at the bottom gate. Ralph (horse) followed Zachariah and Grady followed Ralph (horse) and then started scratching Ralph's belly.

Another choice-point emerged – let this liberty meet continue for another fifteen minutes and dispense with the second part of the experiment (I had planned in my mind) which included brushes for grooming. I decided to introduce the brushes, reasoning that it was likely that Jackson, Zachariah and Grady's attention would waiver soon without some change, but I wanted to do it in a way that didn't interrupt the silence and process that we were experiencing.

I placed the tub of brushes inside the yard and quietly said, "Here are some brushes if you want to use them. Just keep noticing what the horses like and don't like and notice which ones let you know loudly."

"Targeting therapeutic goals around Listening, Communication, Boundary-setting and Relationship skills."

PRACTITIONER OBSERVATIONS:

• Jackson rushed over and picked up several brushes. In stepping back towards Ned (horse), I saw him see Ned's head come up rapidly. He stopped for a second and then walked slowly towards Ned. Ned stood still. Jackson began brushing Ned rapidly. Ned moved away.

• I saw Zachariah watching Jackson. Zachariah was about to pick up a brush, didn't, then walked over to Ned, gesturing to Jackson to follow. Ned stood still. Just as Jimmy had done the previous session, Zachariah put his hand over Jackson's and slowly moved the brush along Ned's belly. No words were spoken.

• Zachariah moved away and Jackson kept brushing. Ned stood still. Zachariah came over and got some brushes. During this time, Grady had picked up a mane brush and was brushing Ralph's long forelock and mane. Then Zachariah went back over to Ollie (horse) and began to brush him, watching Ollie's face the whole time.

• Mabel (horse) began to do the rounds! First, she went to Grady and pushed into his brushing session with Ralph (horse). Grady spent some time brushing her and then Ralph, in turns. Then Mabel turned quickly, flattened her ears and trotted over to Ollie (horse) with her neck out.

• I saw Zachariah notice her approaching and step back. Mabel chased Ollie away and then came back over to Zachariah. Ollie stood about three metres away and began nodding off to sleep immediately.

• Zachariah kind of ignored Mabel and walked back over to Ollie. Again, Mabel rushed over and hunted Ollie away.

• Zachariah walked back over to the bottom gate and was approaching Ned (horse) and Jackson. Jackson said, "Get the fuck away from my horse." The second the words were out, Ned walked away. Jackson and Zachariah watched Ned.

• Zachariah turned and walked over to the brush box and got a different brush and went back over to Ollie (horse). Mabel walked up to Jackson. Jackson started brushing Mabel, but only briefly and then he walked back over to Ned.

When it felt like a natural end, I invited them all to say thank you to the horses and come back out of the yard. Jackson didn't want to come. He was hugging Ned around the neck. Ned was relaxed. A further choice-point – make a deal of Jackson staying in, or just give him time. I chose to give him time.

I asked nobody in particular, "What did you experience?" Jimmy (father) immediately talked about how Mabel was scared of the wire and let everyone know by the way she was moving around.

I offered some observations and said what I had noticed (of Mabel's behaviour and Jimmy's responses) and wondered what he was experiencing. He said he knew she just "needed someone to show her that it wasn't dangerous" and he "just knew that if I walked around to it, she would be happier." He said something like, "Sometimes you just need to show someone that the new thing is safe and then it won't scare them."

Jackson had come out of the yard by now and we just let that sentence sit in the air for a while. It was a choice-point whether to talk more about that at that point, particularly because it sounded like a skill Jimmy has and could easily be named as such. However, I decided not to. The silence seemed more important.

After a time, I said, "Yep, I noticed that Mabel had a lot to say." Zachariah said something like, "She is the one who pushes to get what she wants. She gets jealous. Ollie is like the one that just waits. That's why I like him." I said, "Do you think that's a bit like you, or not like you?" Zachariah said, "Ummmm, like me. Maybe I'm like Ollie." I said, "Hmmm, maybe you're like Ollie." Zachariah was looking at Jackson as we talked.

"So much relationship going on! Between the horses, between the siblings, between each horse-human interaction. The communications were all very 'marked' due to the silence, the non-verbal communications and facial/ body expressions on the horse and boys. This experiencing, of self in relationship, of relationship, is where learning and change is born. The brain, the body, the whole person, is participating in a new life experience – this is the unique value of experiments in psychotherapy. This is the opportunity for re-wiring the brain, re-regulating the nervous system, updating old thinking, belief and behaviour patterns and out of date 'internal relationship models', through new, safe, experience."

"An example of Phenomenological Inquiry which is fundamentally open and curious, with no practitioner agenda to steer or lead the focus of dialogue to practitioners' hypotheses, theories or agenda!"

"Potential emerging themes here for Jimmy around danger, safety, and supporting someone to be safe/know safety, and potentially 'caring for others'. An opportunity for him also to model for his sons - tracking fear/ danger; how to keep someone safe; and how to support others. A skill the father could notice in himself and build on, in time."

"A further choice point and opting with the power of silence. It is important that practitioners assess and know when to talk, when not to talk, and be agile and adaptive, depending on the client process and client needs."

"Here we have an insight into what Zachariah notices, his values and likes, what matters to him, and potentially what he aspires to. Practitioners can further understand the client, their world, perception, values, projections and patterns, as they deeply listen to the clients' responses to the horses and their experience in the EAP session. And then 'check it out' – do you think he's a bit like you, or not like you?'"

Grady spoke into that moment and said something like, "I was scared and then Ralphie stayed with me and I wasn't scared anymore." I said, "Yes, I noticed Ralphie stood with you for a long while and I saw you brush his forelock a lot." Grady said, "He liked it!" I asked him how he knew and he said he kept pointing his face at him. "What was it like?" I asked, and he grinned and said, "GREAT"! I said, "I saw Mabel come over and you started brushing them in turns." And he said, "Yep, she was left out."

Jackson was kicking at the ground a bit while we were talking. A choice-point emerged to make explicit some of my observations of Jackson, and risk including him, or alienating him (if it was perceived as too challenging) or, keep quiet. I decided to take the risk since I had no idea if I would see him again.

I said, "Yeah, I noticed Jackson brushed Mabel for a little while, when she walked up too. Hey Jackson?" He looked up and said, "Yep." Encouraged, I said, "I saw, when you first went in to the yard and started brushing Ned that Ned walked away from you and then I saw you and Zachariah both go over to him and do some brushing and I wondered what that was like?" "OK," he said, "he stood still."

The taxi had arrived (early) and I was aware we needed to wrap up. I asked if they wanted to say goodbye to the horses over the fence quickly, since the taxi was there, and they did. As we walked out, I asked, "Hey, what would you each say if I said to give me ONE word about today, what would you say?"

Grady immediately said, "Horses are the BEST!" and grinned like his face would split.

Zachariah said, "Ollie."

Jackson looked like he wasn't going to say anything, he was walking out the gate. I said, "Jackson?" He turned and looked down. "Just one word?" I asked. "Nice," he said and smiled.

Jimmy walked out last. Stuck his hand out. I shook it. "Thanks, hey. Thanks".

"Grady's emerging themes – feeling frightened and seeking/yearning for support from others. A further potential theme about being supported, included and being left out, might also be relevant for Grady in his life."

"A touch of last minute integration and closure of the session – fitting for the whole flavour of the session being adaptive and 'on the fly'. What a good choice! The practitioner got to hear, and the family had an opportunity to hear how each had experienced the session as enjoyable and potentially significant as a family / relationship experience. Each member had a (new) experience of being safe, having time and space, being heard, learning about relationships and experiencing the fathers' capacity to care and support."

"Zachariah potentially experienced some healthy pride and satisfaction – sharing the horses and his new knowledge and confidence with his family. This session gives such a lovely example of how EPI Model of EAP can be such a great fit for innovative and culturally sensitive psychotherapy with Indigenous clients."

Chapter 6
SAFE STORMY – ADULT WITH COMPLEX TRAUMA

PRACTITIONER INFORMATION

NOEL HAARBURGER is a Psychologist and Gestalt Psychotherapist of over 20 years, Supervisor and Trainer at Gestalt Therapy Australia for 15 years, Somatic Experiencing practitioner and Assistant, Trauma Specialist, and Senior Trainer at The Equine Psychotherapy Institute offering advanced trainings to equine assisted practitioners in working with trauma, the inner critic, nature-based psychotherapy, anxiety, and depression. Noel works in Melbourne in a busy Psychology and Psychotherapy clinical practice, and in country Victoria offering nature-based and equine assisted psychotherapy.

CLIENT BACKGROUND INFORMATION

PLEASE NOTE: *Nick is a pseudonym for the client*

Nick was referred in May 2017. He is 50 year old Australian male who lives alone in country Victoria. He reports having no friends besides occasionally having phone contact with an ex-girlfriend. He is linked into a local welfare support service that supports people with mental health issues. Nick came to see me for trauma informed psychotherapy to help him manage his complex post-traumatic stress symptoms. Some of the symptoms that he initially reported included flashbacks, social anxiety, intrusive memories from his past abuse history, moving between feeling overwhelmed and then numb, a pervasive feeling of being unsafe in the world, regular muscle spasms that felt like epileptic fits, avoiding and fearing people and new situations, fear of feeling and being inside his body, severe social withdrawal and isolation, and feelings of despair, chronic suicidal ideation and hopelessness about ever changing, and enormous self-criticism and shame about his history, believing that he was 'making it all up' or 'making a big deal out of it'.

Over the first year of the psychotherapy work, Nick reported more and more about his early history of severe abuse. He reported that his parents broke up when he was 4 years old, and due to a number of complex factors, ended up going to live with his father, after a bitter custody battle. His paternal grandmother also lived with his father. Nick described his father as controlling, physically violent, sexually and emotionally abusive, and an alcoholic. While he was living with his father, his uncle came to live with him, who was also physically abusive, and ended up sexually abusing him between the ages of 6 to 8 years old. He apparently died when Nick was 9 years old. Nick reported that his father and grandmother knew about the abuse from his Uncle, but did nothing to protect him. Nick had intermittent contact with his mother over this period, and said he felt profoundly abandoned by her. He reported that he has no clear narrative memory of this early abuse, and as a result often believed that it didn't happen, concluding that he was insane and making it all up. This self-doubt was strengthened by complete family denial of the abuse when he later attempted to disclose it to other members of his family. He reported that his father always said he was over-reactive, and regularly gaslighting and making Nick feel wrong. Nick described learning that in order to be safe and avoid his fathers' rage and violence he had to freeze and be compliant and appeasing. He described from as early as he could recall it was dangerous for him to be angry, emotional or stand up for himself.

THERAPEUTIC GOALS

Nick's diagnosis is consistent with complex post-traumatic stress disorder. Therapeutic goals included:

• To build self-regulation resources, to reduce his hyper-active threat response, and constant triggering into somatic and emotional flashbacks.

• To help build capacity for healthier boundaries,

• To differentiate safety from danger

• To down regulate states of high activation and anticipatory social anxiety that get evoked in social situations.

• To over the longer-term, rebuild the capacity to reconnect with his own body awareness to counteract his strong levels of dissociation

• To rebuild some healthy trust in human connection

• To begin to establish an experience of social connection and community, to mitigate his social isolation.

• To identify, investigate and relax his deep core beliefs and convictions that he was wrong and bad, that the world was unsafe and that all people were dangerous, especially men.

• To work explicitly with clients' inner critic as well as the traumatized child parts to support the above goals and re-build a new relationship with himself of deep understanding, capacity and compassion.

BACKGROUND INFORMATION

Despite the level of complex PTSD symptomatology that he was experiencing, Nick was deeply motivated in building his awareness and skills to understand and manage his moods and symptoms. Over the last several years he continued to work on the multiple triggers in his life that evoke extreme anxiety and flashbacks from his past (e.g. facing unfamiliar people, social situations and new environments). Nick has continued to explore his triggers, to understand what they evoke in him and his nervous system from his traumatic past. He reported that he wanted to develop tools (e.g. cognitive capacities, mindfulness, self-compassion, somatic and emotional regulation skills) to soothe these flashbacks, nervous system dysregulation and intense emotions.

After two years of working together in room-based clinical work, I asked Nick if he was willing to try equine assisted psychotherapy to further develop some of the therapeutic goals in a live relationship with horses. He was initially frightened by this invitation but was willing and eager to experience a session. Nick shared he had previously had frightening experiences with horses, reporting one memory where, although not badly hurt, he was knocked over and trampled by a horse as a 9 year old child.

FIRST SESSION

We began our equine assisted psychotherapy session, on a lovely, late summer day, standing outside the horse arena. I had invited our trusty and very grounded mare Stormy, who is one of our oldest and safest horses, aged 27 years. We began the session with some chit chat and then I invited Nick to do an exercise that would support him to arrive and become grounded, through bringing his attention the how his feet connected to the earth. After this process, Nick reported feeling quite settled in some parts of his body (e.g. legs and arms), although there were some anxiety-based sensations in his stomach, which he described as butterflies and tightness. I invited him to touch briefly into these sensations, asking if they were tolerable. He said they were very uncomfortable, but could tell they were tolerable. I asked him how he knew this? He said he wasn't dissociating and was still present. Given that he was still in a window of tolerance, I asked Nick if he was willing to track these fear sensations using somatic mindfulness and to notice what happened next as he watched them with curiosity. To his surprise, within a few minutes he said they had settled even more down to a 2 out of 10 in intensity. When inquiring if he knew what his butterflies were communicating, he said he was feeling anxious and uncertain about how the session would unfold, he was scared of meeting Stormy and had worries something bad would happen. I reassured Nick that we would go slowly and gently, and that we wouldn't do anything unless he wanted to, holding the intention to give him as much agency and control as possible in the session. I reminded him that he was in control of how much contact he wanted to have with Stormy today and that he could choose to interact with Stormy from behind the fence, for the whole session, if he preferred.

I offered Nick the safety guideline, further informing him about horses, what would happen, how

"Our EPI Model supports clients to become aware, grounded and regulated before connecting directly with the horses. This includes some important trauma-informed practices of breathing, grounding, orienting and resourcing, which are essential supports for working with clients with histories of developmental trauma"

"Trauma-informed practices support clients to practice working with interoception (bringing attention to sensations in the body) and nervous system mapping (learning to detect the current state of the nervous system e.g. signals of sympathetic nervous system activation or dorsal vagal shut down), titration (supporting clients' to experience only a drop of disturbing or activation sensations, that is tolerable) and, explicitly working with the clients' window of tolerance (Dan Seigel, 2010)."

"We invite clients to scale or rate their activation levels, and feelings, in EPI model sessions, so clients can start to track, self-assess and build resources and capacities with intentionality (to use outside of the session)."

"This is an awareness practice tool we include in our EPI model work that focuses on the information, message or need that sensations or feelings may be communicating."

to keep himself safe and retain further agency and choice in the session.

I invited Nick to orient to Stormy from behind the fence and describe what he noticed. Stormy was standing about 10 feet away from him, chewing on some hay. Nick noticed that Stormy was eating, but said he wasn't sure if she was relaxed or not. We discussed some of the features of relaxed body language and tracked Stormy's positioning, muscle tone, breath and behaviour. I observed and shared with Nick some horse observations as Stormy had a leg cocked, soft eyes, forward ears, relaxed muscles, was eating hay and rhythmically licking and chewing. Nick observed and listened, although looked hesitant and vigilant in his facial expression. The purpose of this conversation was to help Nick re-build a more balanced neuroception. Neuroception is a term coined by Stephen Porges, which describes our wired in innate biological capacity to notice cues of danger and safety. One of the common impacts of trauma is that neuroception becomes maladaptive and overly skewed towards noticing cues of threat and missing cues of safety. My intention was to help Nick redevelop his neuroceptive skills and capacity towards also consciously noticing cues of safety.

I asked Nick if there was something that he wanted to work on in the session or get out of the session for the day. He said that he wanted to explore the theme of connection; what gets in the way of it and what might support him to establish more connection in his life to address his loneliness. After unpacking this, the theme that arrived most clearly was Nick's yearning to be able to connect, but his terror of it. With this theme in mind, I considered that a good experiment would simply be make contact with Stormy in a way that felt right to Nick. I invited Nick if he was willing to come into the arena and stand at about 3 meters away from Stormy, letting him know that he could make contact with Stormy in any way that felt right to him. Nick said he would like to. However, when

"An important part of the Check In and initial phase of psychotherapy including assessing therapeutic goals and soft contracting around agreed focus for the session. The emergent theme of exploring connection, yearning to connect and obstacles to connection arrived."

"The assessment and soft contracting inform the development of the Experiment (in gestalt terms), in this case in the context of EAP - the relational experience with the horse that supports the exploration of the clients' emergent themes (around connection). The experiment brings the themes 'to life' by exploring, experiencing and experimenting in the here and now, ensuring the learning is not just a cognitive exercise, rather a whole body, brain, behaviour and relational discovery."

I invited him to scan his body again and to report on the intensity of his nervous system activation, using a rating scale from 0-10, Nick reported that he was now feeling about 8 out of 10. I asked him how he knew he was activated, and he said his heart was racing and he was feeling shaky and adrenalized. I suggested that he was going into a high sympathetic nervous system state, and invited him to stop and just reconnect to one of the resources that we had named in the beginning of the session (in the regulation and resourcing exercise). My intention was to help Nick strengthen his capacity to notice and build flexibility to come out of sympathetic activation via learning to monitor his arousal and pendulate his attention to something that would bring his nervous system back to regulation (also known as a ventral vagal anchor). Nick said bringing his attention to his feet and focusing on the sound of the leaves gently moving in the trees was comforting and his activation began to settle. I asked Nick to also notice any signals of safety in Stormy, and invited him to share what he saw. Nick said he wasn't sure. Nick also said he was worried that he would somehow violate Stormy, and that he was concerned Stormy was appeasing us and wouldn't like it if he was to move closer and make contact.

I asked Nick to be curious about this statement, and reassured him that Stormy, being at liberty, could walk away from Nick at any point if she wanted. Nick all of a sudden said, "I think this is what I do". I asked him what he meant. Nick said "I am always worried about being violated and tend to appease people or withdraw in order to stay safe". With this insight, Nick expressed sadness and grief at the realization that it was him that was scared, not Stormy, and that he was projecting his abused self into Stormy. I invited Nick to stay with his grief and allow it to be there. He said he was willing to do this and took a few minutes to be present to his feelings. After a few minutes, Nick appeared settled again.

"Our trauma-informed EPI approach means that we include somatic experiencing and nervous state assessment as an essential tool to support clients'. From a Polyvagal theory perspective (S. Porges and Deb Dana) we want our clients to assess when they are in ventral vagal, sympathetic or dorsal vagal states, and support over-time, flexibility and capacity across all 3 states of the nervous system. The client was in high sympathetic arousal state rating it an 8 out of 10!"

"Here, the practitioner is building the clients neuroceptive capacity by helping him orient to resources and asking him to assess the nervous state of the horse (who was in rest and digest or ventral vagal nervous state of relaxation and connection)."

"What a powerful moment for the client to notice this projection, and remain openly curious. This was also an example using the paradoxical theory of change in gestalt therapy, which purports that when we stay present to our experiential intensity (with enough resources) it naturally changes."

81

Again I invited him to see if he was willing to take a step towards Stormy, and if at any point he noticed his body becoming activated, he could stop and take some time to re-regulate until he was settled. We ended up doing this over the next 40 minutes!

Each time Nick took a step towards Stormy, his body became significantly activated e.g. increased heart rate and body constriction, and he would stop and then practice grounding, out breaths and orienting to safe cues in the horse, in myself (practitioner) and in the environment.

I asked Nick what was going through his mind when he took another step towards Stormy, who was still eating hay. He said he was still worried and hesitant that she wouldn't like him and want contact. At some point, Stormy walked away to the other end of the arena. I asked Nick what this was like for him. He said that he expected this would happen. I asked him if this was familiar to him. He said that he was always expecting rejection or aggression from people, and had learnt to withdraw and isolate to stay safe. I listened too and validated Nicks feelings in the context of his abuse history, reflecting back to him that it made sense that being mistrustful was a way he learnt to stay safe. I suggested to Nick that if he wanted a relationship with Stormy he might have to initiate contact and experiment with being more pro-active and learning what was true, in the here and now (rather than generalising and projecting). Nick said this was extremely unfamiliar, but was willing to experiment with doing this, with my support.

Over the next 30 minutes, I invited Nick to experiment with making contact with Stormy, again at his pace. We went over a few more rounds of him taking a step towards Stormy, tracking his activation levels using the scale, and stopping to re-regulating his nervous system whenever he needed. As a way to support him, I asked Nick if he would be open to seeing me make contact with Stormy and noticing

"This is an important part of trauma practice, to invite the client to experience small amounts of activation (or sympathetic nervous state arousal), but with new supports – of co-regulation (of practitioner and horse), choice, agency, and building flexibility across all nervous system states."

"Another important emergent theme – others won't like me or want relationship signalling a deeper introject (belief) perhaps around I am not likeable."

"Here, the horses' role in the session and contribution to clients' process moves from being an initial disturbance of the homeostasis and 'unsafe other', to co-regulator, to evoking and triggering feelings and patterns."

"Change requires new supports – self supports and external supports (including safe others)."

"Experiments, practice and repetition is the key to build new neural firings and neural circuits in the brain, new felt sense memories, new awareness (not just insight) and new patterns of thinking and behaving (similar to behaviour modification principles and practices, however, with increased tracking and open curiosity in the interventions)."

how Stormy responds. When we were within a few feet of Stormy, I demonstrated touching Stormy and noticing her response. Stormy continued to show signals of being regulated, had a softness in her eyes, a cocked leg and continued chewing. I shared with Nick again that these were signals of regulation and safety and that, from my experience, indicated she was in a relaxed state and receptive to contact. Eventually, with a lot of trepidation, Nick reached out to pat Stormy a few times. I asked him what he noticed in himself and Stormy when he did this. He said he could see that Stormy was still looking relaxed, and that he could feel his body relaxing too. I invited him to do it again, and to experiment with what kind of touch Stormy liked, by watching her body language and again noticing the cues of her being relaxed and safe. Nick tried patting Stormy on the withers and forehead, and at some point, she turned her head towards Nick and gently nuzzled him in the chest. I noticed that Nicks face beamed with a smile and looked visibly bright and alive. I shared my observation and asked Nick what he experienced. He said that he was feeling his whole body de-constrict. I asked him if he was willing to just track the effects of this de-constriction in his body and to see what else he noticed. After another few minutes Nick reported that his breath had deepened and his heart rate felt slow. He said he was really surprised that he felt relaxed being in contact with Stormy, and that he expected something different.

"Extra support, modelling and continual 'nudging' in the experimenting – where the practitioner (in the context of a longer term therapeutic relationship with the client) risks influencing and nudging, demonstrating a belief in the clients' potential for change)."

"Constant and continual tracking and invitation for the client to share their subjective experience and nervous state in this session."

"Continual phenomenological observations and phenomenological inquiry is the main therapeutic approach alongside the stream of experimenting and reflecting."

INTEGRATION PHASE

Given that we were almost out of time, I asked him what this meant to him and what he might be taking away today from his experience with Stormy. Nick said, he realized more clearly that he tends to expect danger to be all around him, and that he could see it is his fearful part, a legacy of his early trauma, that stops him from recognizing any evidence of safety and connection now. He said that his fear is not always accurate. He said he always assumed that because he is scared, the environment must be dangerous. I offered Nick some psycho-education on neuroception (a term coined by Stephen Porges that describes our sub-psychological awareness of danger and safety) and how it is often skewed by trauma – one experiences and expects danger, even when it is actually (now) safe. Nick nodded and said he now understands this! He shared he was now able to recognize that Stormy was not dangerous, and to recognize the cues of safety. I asked "how do you know?". He said he can see she is not walking away, that her eyes are soft and that 'she wants to be with him'. Nick also said it was scary for him to let go of his trauma map, and notice cues of safety, as it meant loosening up his old survival strategy of mistrust and expecting danger (a familiar state). He said the trauma map was familiar and known, and that learning to be open and to trust, made him feel disoriented, vulnerable and scared. This was his disturbance and dilemma.

"It is disturbing and a vulnerable place, to risk change!"

REFLECTION AFTER THE SESSION

After this session with Nick, I was reminded of how relational trauma shapes and distorts our neuroception towards looking for and expecting danger, and the many ways that this hyper-*orientation to danger* is a survival and protective mechanism to keep us from being hurt or harmed again. I was left in awe of Nicks courage to face and sit with his fears, and to take risks to make contact with Stormy despite his trauma-shaped fears.

Stormy gave Nick many opportunities - the opportunity to face the sensations in his body that go with fear; to learn to monitor and modify his nervous system states; to work experientially with his nervous system activation, feelings and cognitions; and ultimately, to *experience* something new in our sessions that had not been possible in the room-based sessions. Having his experience of fear evoked in such a palpable and consistent way in the session gave him repeated experiences of not just reflecting on his fear, nervous system and accompanying cognitive-behavioural patterns, but, exploring, experimenting and facing it directly, experientially. Nick learnt that he can track and be present to his interoceptive and subjective experience, and, he can recognize the difference between danger and safety in his current environment. Stormy offered the opportunity to have Nicks fears and old trauma generated beliefs evoked, and then disconfirmed through building a positive and safe connection with Stormy. Stormy gave Nick the opportunity to update his file! This began the next focus in our sessions together, and over the next several sessions we explored more with Stormy about how to build connection and trust in relationships.

"Experiencing in the here and now is a core principle of the AWARE TherapyTM approach, offering clients the opportunity to gain awareness of their patterns, test fixed ways of thinking or behaving, challenge outdated patterns or beliefs or, as it suggests, experience a new way of being or doing, without over analysing."

"One of the reasons why we believe EAP is clinically so effective!"

Chapter 7

RESOURCING WITH TOTO –
ADULT RIDING PERSONAL
DEVELOPMENT SESSION

PRACTITIONER INFORMATION

MAELANI MILLS is a new EAL practitioner having certified in 2020 and has a specialist business named Equine Ananda, meaning "Alchemy of the Horse & Human Spirit".

Being a registered Yoga teacher and mindset coach, Mae is passionate about personal growth and development, and Mae has been offering unique horse assisted yoga sessions for the last four years.

Mae enjoyed the EAL training journey with the Institute so much, she has become inspired about counselling and psychotherapy with horses! Mae has now enrolled in a Counselling diploma, with a view to certifying and offering EAP in the near future.

CLIENT BACKGROUND INFORMATION

PLEASE NOTE: *Erica is a pseudonym for the client*

Erica is in her early 30s, a busy mum of two young boys, currently studying naturopathy as well as running a small business. Erica is feeling stressed with school decisions, running a household, and has limited time for self-care.

Erica mentioned that her husband has a love of horses and she dreamed that one day she could fearlessly go on a ride with him. Erica experienced seeing someone fall off a horse on a TV show and has been afraid of horses ever since. She has no pets and lives in an urban suburb of Melbourne.

Erica was drawn to book a session because of her interest in yoga, however, she also had dual focus to face her fear of horses. Erica wanted to participate in a single session and then make plans to perhaps have fortnightly sessions from there-on-in.

The learning focus and learning goals included:

• Regulating and resourcing the client

• Providing a safe relationship

• Increasing awareness and re-connect with nature

SESSION

In my preparation, because of Erica's strong desire to sit on a horse, I planned to work towards a mounted experience in our session. However, I also kept in mind that Erica was unfamiliar with horses, so I would need to track and observe her and the horse, to gauge suitability on the day.

As I do not currently have my own property, I arrived early to spend some time with Toto, my 7-year-old Warmblood gelding in the paddock. We then walked around the arena, where I could track his mood and notice any signs of stress or non-consent. Toto has a retroflection pattern, so I'm generally on the lookout for his subtle signs of clenched jaw/lips, tail swishing, dull eyes, high neck etc. He appeared relaxed and willing.

I met with Erica in the car park and had a chat before meeting any horses. She said she was really nervous and had never been next to a horse before, let alone touched one! I explained that our sessions are experiential, led by the horse's consent, and that we would focus the first session on feeling more comfortable being in the presence of horses, on the ground, first and foremost, with a mounted option in the future.

I introduced Erica to Toto on the lead-line. She appeared frightened and uncomfortable being close to him, especially when he would move or stomp at flies. She was jumpy. I immediately decided to take the idea of a mounted experience out of the equation, as it felt too much, too soon.

We spent 10 minutes tuning into outbreath, grounding and awareness. A body scan revealed that Erica was holding a lot of tension in her chest which she named as fear. Her breath was shallow and her chest felt constricted and heavy. She found that tuning inwards and focusing on how her body was feeling, eased this tension and brought more lightness with each outbreath.

I invited Erica to move closer to Toto and, if in her window of tolerance, to place her hand on his shoulder. Her eyes were wide and she appeared hesitant but once she connected with him, she took an outbreath and her shoulders and face were less guarded and tense. I encouraged her to continue to touch Toto and move around him as long as it felt safe for the both of them. Toto softened his eyes further and I continued to track both horse and client. I noticed that Erica was much more visibly relaxed, now with a smile on her face.

"This is a Gestalt Therapy 'contact style' (unaware relationship pattern) which is defined generally as a tendency to hold back or hold in, and not move to spontaneous expression. This tendency in humans and horses, can lead to holding breath, tensing or contracting in the body, not saying how they feel. People or horses with this behavioural pattern can appear "fine" but underneath, may actually feel stressed, have feelings or wants that they are not freely expressing or chronically suppressing."

"This is an example of the paradoxical theory of change – tuning into what is happening in the here and now, noticing, naming and welcoming the fear, is what supports a shift or change into another experience (that arrives organically, once the feeling has been noticed, named and accepted). Fear and tension are accepted, then, lightness and ease arrives. This is very different to a solution focused approach to change, which may, for example, move the focus to the 'ideal' or 'desired state' i.e. confidence and calm, and attempt to create that feeling or state without experiencing or exploring the actual experiential truth, in the moment, fear."

After a couple of minutes, I invited Erica to face Toto's side, ground down squarely into her feet and place her hands, with open palms, on Toto's upper back. She focused on her breath and sensations in her body as she exhaled. We then brought her awareness to Toto's breathing and encouraged her to match her own breath with his, noticing and feeling his belly contract and expand. She then closed her eyes and continued to ground and breathe. Toto remained still with his head and neck held low and relaxed.

I then asked Erica to stand next to Toto's shoulder, facing me, and we moved through a gentle yoga flow. I encouraged her to ground down into all four corners of her feet and notice the feeling of being completely supported by the Earth. I invited her to close down her eyes and tune into all the other senses, one by one.

When she opened her eyes, I encouraged her to focus on peripheral vision, taking in the full surroundings, as the horses do. We then moved with breath through a standing flow (sun salutations) as Toto stood beside her. She noticed his energy and remarked that it was powerful yet comforting.

I then asked Erica how she was feeling now. She said she felt both energised and grounded. The tension in her chest had alleviated and she felt genuinely safe with Toto. I observed that both horse and client were calm and the energy felt peaceful.

I then offered an invitation for Erica to lead Toto, which she accepted enthusiastically. I encouraged her to focus on outbreaths and to continue to express her felt sense of calmness through her hands, on the lead, to Toto. She held the lead rope loosely and walked around the arena, Toto held his head low and walked along at the same pace beside her. Occasionally they would stop and Toto would prick his ears and use his mouth to explore her arm. Erica welcomed his playfulness and smiled.

"First experiment offered was the Touching experiment, and the second experiment, the Tracking and Matching her breath with the horse's breath. These were good initial experiment choices to support the client to slowly and safely work towards her learning goals, regulating, resourcing, increasing awareness, re-connecting with nature, and facing her fear of horses."

"This next experiment appears to be a nicely graded experiment, allowing for a little more of a stretch, given that the client had already widened her window of tolerance for her fear, and increased her felt sense of resourcing."

Upon check-in, Erica said she felt very connected and drawn to Toto and that she could never have imagined feeling so comfortable with a horse. The tension in her chest had shifted to warmth and joy.

At this point in observing and tracking both horse and client, I felt open and keen to offer a mounted experience to end our session. I asked how the prospect of sitting on Toto felt in her body. She said that it gave her a rush of sensation in her chest, but this time, instead of the fear, it was more a feeling of nervous excitement.

To stay connected with Erica's feeling of being grounded and present, we then moved through a short yoga warrior sequence with a focus on breath, opening up the hips and stretching the legs. I guided her through a chest opening pose to encourage expansiveness and an open-heart space before mounting Toto.

As she stood on the mounting block, I invited Erica to focus on her outbreaths. I briefly explained how she could slide herself on to Toto's back and encouraged her to confidently move through the motion entirely, to sitting on his back. Toto is sensitive to people who are visibly nervous and linger in the half on, half off space but today he showed no concern or objection (through his body language) as Erica was fluid and confident.

Once mounted, Erica mentioned she noticed a rush of sensation through her body. Without guidance, she appeared to regulate herself with outbreaths and tension release. I encouraged her to notice her body and relax the areas she was holding on to, particularly in her shoulders and hips.

I encouraged her to continue to connect with Toto through touch and to express her outbreaths and calm energy through her hands and body. Toto remained at ease with floppy ears, soft eyes and a lowered head. He appeared to be very responsive to Erica's regulating and I did not notice any concern in him through the

"As well as being a wonderful yoga sequence, this is also a fantastic preparation for the client to become more aware, preparing her body, legs and hips to mount and sit on the horse's wide barrel, and generally supporting her presence and readiness to step further into intimacy with the horse, Toto."

entire session. All his body language appeared to be congruent with communication signals of regulation, relaxation and consent.

I stayed silent for the most part of the mounted experience, besides inviting her to experience Toto walking, which she smiled and accepted. As the mounted experience came to an end, I invited Erica to thank Toto in a way that felt safe and right for both Toto and herself. She leaned forward and gave Toto a full embrace, with arms around his neck, completely supported by him. Again, Toto remained relaxed in his body and behaviour, and appeared to be in consent of Erica's arms and body around him.

This session appeared to meet the client's learning goals well – supported the client by increasing her awareness, focusing on further developing self supports, offered a unique experience of safe relationship, culminating in (step by step) facing her generalised fears of horses.

Erica mentioned that continuing to focus on how her body felt, took the focus off her mind's thoughts about the fear, where she had been stuck. The fears were not fear, per se, but rather *worried thoughts* or catastrophe-based thinking and *cognitive patterns*.

Erica explained that because she was so in tune with soaking up the experience of the present moment, her thoughts did not cloud or dominate her experience. She was able to address her fear by focusing on her body and Toto, rather than get hijacked by the out of date, or out of touch with reality, thoughts that had become stuck in her mind.

"Our EPI Model Led Mounted sessions include a focus on the horses' phenomenology, as a part of the intervention and bio-feedback mechanism, and, consent. EPI practitioners are looking for body language from the horse that is congruent with a 'yes' 'this is OK with me' (to have this person on my back) through a combination of regulated, relaxed and expressive body language. The led mounted sessions include the horses' consent, feelings and expressions, moment to moment. This shapes the trajectory, content and process of the session."

REFLECTION

Upon reflection of her experience, Erica said she was surprised that she was able to stay completely *in the moment* and never once thought about the things happening in her life that normally consumed her thoughts each day.

She felt energised, refreshed, and for the first time in a while, the typically constant experience of worry or anxiety was gone. She then made a commitment to continue doing these things, for herself, as she realised how important they were to her wellbeing.

Upon reflection of this session, I believe that Toto was the key contributor to client change. He offered co-regulation, confirmation, and a deeply somatic (body-based) experience to unfold as it did. Horse and client appeared to co-regulate each other throughout the session, and Toto appeared to relax further when Erica matched his breathing and focused on letting down with each exhale.

Erica responded positively to Toto's calmness and settled nervous system, and she noted the calming effect he had on her. Being able to touch and be held by Toto, emotionally and physically, appeared to heighten Erica's sense of embodiment, attunement and intimacy in relationship. She appeared to relax and become more comfortable, the more contact she had with him.

I personally gained a lot of insight from observing Erica in this session. She began in a high state of fear and anxiousness which quickly dissipated the more grounded, present, and aware she became. I have worked with many nervous clients but this experience went from a highly fearful state to a place of trust in an overall short amount of time. It was beautiful to observe this session unfold naturally and organically without much guidance, just in being there to support her to build this connection with Toto.

No matter how well I think I know my horses, there is always more to learn about them as individuals in every session. Toto normally picks up on fear and nervousness quickly, which then turns to uncertainty and cautiousness in him. However, in this session,

"Important for practitioners to be continually reflecting on how the horse supported change in the client, in each session. What were the qualities, interactions, or triggers that contributed to client change today? This is something that is central to our approach at the Institute, we never want to assume the horse's role, but rather stay alert, aware, tracking and openly curious about the horses' role – this keeps practitioners current and continually developing their practice and understanding of EAL as an effective modality."

"There is actually a lot going on, on the inside (of the practitioners' foundation skills and competencies), and yet it appears there is not a lot happening. This is the art of masterful facilitation."

he remained calm and relaxed, and he was the true teacher in this experience!

This session really encouraged my growth as an EAL practitioner. I was able to successfully bracket any personal judgments or concerns of this client's fear, the concern that it would transfer to the horse, and allow the experience to transpire in a truly authentic and organic way.

Erica was able to have a full cycle of experience with Toto, without any interference from my fears, my concerns or assumptions impacting my attitude, presence and interventions.

I enjoyed trusting the process, and letting the session authentically happen. I went with my intuition to offer more than I had originally expected, which gave more depth to the experience and allowed the client to achieve one of her main goals of feeling comfortable on and around a horse.

" *We honour our patterns as intelligent solutions that we developed to self-protect, maintain attachment or support survival in the past...that are now out-of-date.* "

MEG KIRBY

Chapter 8

LEWIS ON THE TRAIL – ADOLESCENT WITH COMPLEX TRAUMA AND VIOLENCE

PRACTITIONER INFORMATION

NADINE is a Mental Health Social Worker working in the Hunter Valley, NSW. Nadine specialises in working with children and adolescents with complex needs, including autism, range of intellectual capacity, and diverse clinical diagnoses and presentations.

Nadine is the Director of Hunter Valley Children's Therapies, which is a full time equine assisted psychotherapy business, providing services to young people across the beautiful Hunter Valley district and beyond.

Hunter Valley Children's Therapies is always full, and maintains a wait list, as the services are much needed in the community and in high demand. Nadine relishes the opportunity to support young people to develop essential life skills, providing an environment that facilitates full expression of the unique children she works with, ensuring they experience a safe relational container to reach towards their potential.

CLIENT INFORMATION

PLEASE NOTE: *Kate is a pseudonym for the client*

Kate has been diagnosed with Post Traumatic Stress Disorder with associated Generalized Anxiety Disorder, Attention Deficit Hyperactivity Disorder (combined type) and Specific Learning Disorder (written expression).

CLIENT BACKGROUND

Kate has a history of severe abuse and neglect. She was removed from her young mother, who had chronic dependency issues and often left her infant unsupervised for extended lengths of time. Now aged 14 years, Kate is living in out of home care, and is currently in a residential care placement. Kate has a history of being very violent in out of home care placements and at school, and has had limited school attendance. Kate struggles with trust in relationships and periodically has suicidal ideation.

Kate is a very bright girl, and has a great deal of insight. She has been attending EAP for approximately a year and expresses that she loves coming to sessions. She always appears very engaged, verbally expressive, and shares that she enjoys the 'therapy' aspects of sessions.

Kate's therapeutic goals include providing safety in relationship, building sense of self, resourcing and regulating her nervous system, providing Kate with a safe environment for disclosure, expression of feelings and needs, and safely processing traumatic memories as they emerge.

ORIENTING TO THE SESSION

In the previous session, Kate and I had discussed the opportunity to trail ride in the following session, as this had been a long-term goal that in the beginning was very much 'out of reach' as she felt too frightened to even imagine riding (even though she dearly wanted to).

After a year of ground-based EAP sessions together, the time had come, and at Kate's instigation, for a mounted EAP experience.

Mounted EAP sessions can offer clients a variety of experiences and potential benefits including:

• A safe and supportive relational experience of being held by an 'other'.

• The rhythmic, rocking motion of the horse's walk can assist in soothing the brain stem and nervous system.

• The physical contact with the horse by large parts of the body, like the hips, buttocks and legs, can offer deep muscle pressure, which provides input into the sensory system, offering feelings of relaxation and aid in the release of serotonin.

• For those with trauma, the somatic experience of the rhythm, the physical connection and the sensation of being held, can help re-wire feelings of 'safety' and 'joy'. In general, contact with horses also offers safe, physical touch, which is something that can be lacking for young people in out of home care, where there might be limitations on the physical contact and affection between the carer and the young person. Kate seems to, in every EAP session, seek out and enjoy the physical contact with the horses. She very much appears to enjoy cuddling and patting all of the horses and ponies.

"Whilst this experiment may be selected with the client in mind, exploring a familiar trail may also satisfy enrichment needs for horses who feel safe enough to do so. This is another key AWARE TherapyTM principle practitioners can consider when designing experiments with enrichment for horses (and clients!) in mind."

"This is a nice summary of some of the more unique benefits of mounted or riding based EAP (which of course is not hippotherapy (focusing on physiological benefits of riding), and is not therapeutic riding (which is not delivered by a therapist, psychotherapist or allied / mental health practitioner, and usually focuses on the generalised therapeutic benefit of riding for people with disabilities or people with a range of cognitive or physical abilities). EAP is of course, as it states, psychotherapy with horses that focuses on the psycho-therapeutic goals of the client including feeling held, regulating the nervous system in safe relationship, releasing serotonin and stress responses, re-wiring or re-negotiating one's relationship to joy and safety in relationship, safe touch and other attachment-based, psychological needs of each unique client providing a 'corrective' experience (ie where clients can have unmet developmental needs for safety, holding, movement, touch, food, love and boundaries, met in a psychotherapeutic setting)."

MOUNTED SESSION

I prepared my suitable horse, Lewis, by checking in with him and bringing him into the yard. This way he was close-by, relaxing and eating hay, and ready for the session to begin. Kate arrived with her support worker (from supported accommodation) Celia, as we had agreed that Celia may benefit from seeing what Kate was doing in EAP sessions, and Kate had shared that she was building a very safe and trusting relationship with Celia and was interested in having Celia present during some of the session.

As we were preparing the tack, Kate said that today had been her first full day at school and she had really enjoyed that. This has been something that she has been working towards. She said that she has some struggles with some of the other young people but had managed to avoid getting angry and hadn't assaulted anyone or damaged any property. She appeared proud of this, and I joined in congratulating her, and reflected back that she appeared very pleased with her own progress.

Together, we quietly groomed and saddled Lewis, who appeared very relaxed, with soft eyes and cocked leg, appearing to enjoy the touch and contact with Kate and myself.

Once Kate had mounted, I noticed that her legs were wobbling. I asked Kate what she was feeling. She said that she was feeling nervous. I asked her what her thoughts were and she said she was having thoughts of falling off and the horse rolling on top of her. I offered Kate some supports to regulate her fear, and together we did some breathing exercises.

After a little time, she suggested that she felt ready to move into a walk. So, together we began the walk into the bush track. I was on the ground walking on foot and Kate was mounted and riding alongside me. As we walked down the hill, she expressed nervousness about going down the decline and then back up the incline on the other side.

"Mounted or Ridden EAP requires practitioners to have a safe, well trained horse (trained under saddle), who commonly says 'yes' to having a person on their back (mounting and riding). Practitioners at the Institute are trained to watch for the horses' yes and no, their consent, before proceeding to integrating mounted EAP into their practice repertoire or equine experiments. This is a very important part of the practice ethics, of including animals into psychotherapy process."

"This is very important that Kate is tracking her own behaviour at school, sharing it with her safe support workers, and feeling some healthy pride about the changes she is making in her life."

"This is important for clients to put words to their experience, see how their thoughts impact their feelings, and (with the practitioners support) can choose to re-regulate with using breath or other techniques, if the feelings are too intense. Clients can over-time, learn how to do this when at home, which is incredibly important for agency and capacity building."

I felt that it was an opportunity to support Kate to listen to her fear, and also listen to the message that the fear was offering her, so she could further develop her somatic awareness and emotional awareness. I chose to share some psycho-education at this point to support Kate. I shared that perhaps her fear was her body's way of telling her to be prepared for danger, to encourage her to listen to and trust her body. I did also notice that even though she was saying that she felt fear and nervousness, she was at the same time, smiling. So, I shared this observation and checked in with what was actually happening for her. She shared that sometimes she feels frightened on the inside but finds it a bit overwhelming and doesn't want others to really see her fear and vulnerability. I thanked her for risking sharing this with me, as she clearly felt safe enough to share this with me, which felt like a clear demonstration of the trust she had developed in me and in our relationship.

I continued to offer Kate a lot of support by asking her to use her breath and a grounding exercise to regulate her nervous system and bring her fear into a manageable range. This seemed to work very well. Kate shared that she was enjoying the ride with Lewis, even though it felt frightening at times, she said she felt also supported by my presence and by Lewis, holding her safely, as we all walked together.

By the end of the session, Kate started to appear more and more tired, and even drowsy. So, we gently and carefully dismounted, said thankyou and goodbye to Lewis, and supported Kate into the car. I had noticed that this is a pattern for her in previous EAP sessions, that at around the 45 minute mark of the session, she seems to lose concentration. Out of home care workers have remarked that she often falls asleep on the way home in the car. I wondered if she is experiencing a sense of deep relaxation after having contact with the horses.

"This is a nice awareness that Kate was able to name, that she smiles as a management strategy to cope with feeling frightened, vulnerable and yet unsafe or unsure if it's safe enough for her to share her true experience. Of course, in her history, it was not safe to do so. However now, Kate can start to notice when it is safe in her relational environment, to share more of her truth to certain people. Building her trust in herself, her choice and agency and in some, safe others in her life."

"The mounted EAP session allowed the fear to be regulated, processed and supported in an engaging way."

"It can be exhausting for the nervous system to move out of sympathetic arousal into a more ventral state or state of regulation!"

REFLECTION

As a complex trauma client, Kate seems to live in a fairly constant state of hypervigilance and hyperarousal, where her nervous system is constantly activated, and I would imagine this is exhausting for her. It appears to me her contact and experiences with the horses may have been co-regulating, an opportunity for her nervous system to discharge some of the tension and for her body to feel safe and relaxed. This feeling is possibly unfamiliar to her (and her nervous system).

It is encouraging to see that she has been able to find her sessions resourcing and physiologically regulating. Hopefully, we can create some new neuro-pathways around safety, and safely being in relationship, for her with continual repetition. It is not a short-term fix that we are looking at, rather a longer-term focus on regulating her nervous system and allowing Kate to experience some continuity that life is now safe, good and nourishing at times, and that relationship can be safe and fulfilling.

This will take a long time for her brain-body-whole being to develop this new template for life and relationships. This is very satisfying for me as a practitioner, to imagine being a part of creating a new here and now experience, and future, for Kate.

"Core AWARE Therapy™ principles of resourcing, regulating and safe relationship have all been explored in this session. Whilst complex trauma requires long-term and ongoing support, one can see how many therapeutic outcomes can be addressed through this unique model, incorporating horses and the natural world."

"I believe it is important that clinicians do not get hi-jacked by the popularity of short term therapy, as many complex trauma clients need ongoing work over months and years, and some need therapeutic support for their life span, if the early abuse and neglect was chronic and severe. We are herd animals after all, and are not designed to heal and grow by ourselves. Kate will benefit from Nadine's long-term commitment to their very important work together."

"Awareness gives us Choice to Respond. With No Awareness, we have No Choice, and will React (on automatic pilot)."

MEG KIRBY

Chapter 9
BOUNDARY LESSONS FROM THE HERD - ADULT ADDICTIONS RECOVERY GROUP

PRACTITIONER
INFORMATION

LOUISE ATKINSON is an Equine Assisted Psychotherapist and Learning Practitioner based in Western Australia at the Whispering Sands Horse Play Centre. Louise has been a Horsemanship Instructor for over twenty years. Six years ago, Louise changed direction, trained in Equine Assisted Psychotherapy at the Institute. At this time, she also qualified as a counsellor. Louise's business, Whispering Sands, now offers counselling and psychotherapy to individuals and groups, supporting growth and wellness with horses.

ORIENTING INFORMATION

Whispering Sands offers a 10-week Addictions Recovery Support Program with men suffering with substance and alcohol addiction. Each week there is a different personal development topic designed to help the participants develop skills in self-regulation, coping strategies and become aware of thoughts, feelings, patterns and habits that may not be serving them so well.

A local recovery house attends this program 2-3 times a year. The house consists of 6-10 men of all ages, from late teens to 50+ years, needing support as they recover from their addictions of mostly meth or alcohol. Quite often these men have either a lot of fear, anger and grief bottled up inside. Since the house program requires a minimum of 6 months living together in shared rooms, the men, understandably, have a lot of boundary issues to negotiate. Noticing and Communicating boundaries is an important part of their EAP program.

PLEASE NOTE: *Pseudonyms have been used for clients in this case study*

HERD

Our herd are all male (geldings) and very large horses varying in size from 15.2hh to 18.2hh. Just being in their presence inspires most people to become present to what is happening inside and around them.

SESSION 1

BOUNDARIES

The first session on boundaries. We invite the participants to explore both their own boundaries and/or the horses' boundaries. One of the guys, Tom, walked straight up to one of the horses (Rocky) who promptly responded by pinning his ears back, stretching his head and neck out and moving towards Tom slightly. Tom ignored the horse's body language, behaviour, and the horse's communications with him.

Tom then tried to touch Rocky. Rocky increased his communications, pinning his ears, stretching his neck and head out and finally bared his teeth towards Tom. I swiftly intervened (to ensure Tom was safe, and to invite some curiosity in him about what he was noticing and not noticing about the horses' communications).

I asked Tom to step away from Rocky, and, to get curious about what Rocky *could be* telling him. Tom said that Rocky didn't look happy. I inquired further, also asking about what led him to continue trying to touch Rocky even though Rocky was clearly saying "No", and warning him not to come any closer (through his overt body language). Tom said he thought it was funny.

I inquired further into Tom's experience of 'thinking it funny'. I asked if this was just with the horse, Rocky, or if this was something that had happened before in his life? Has he experienced someone saying 'No' or expressing boundaries 'don't come any closer', and if he tended to ignore their 'No's (or expression of their feelings or boundaries?). He said he did also tend to do this with people, on reflection. I asked Tom, "How does this work out for you?" Apparently not too well, as Tom replied, "I have copped a few beatings."

He went on to share further that he does not have many friends. I listened. Upon further inquiry he said he had been utilising this kind of behaviour (finding other people's feelings and wants as funny, ignoring their personal space boundaries) since he was a child, *trying to get attention*. This was an important insight that had arrived for Tom.

I invited him to experiment again, in relationship with Rocky. This time, explore the possibility of taking a little more time with Rocky, taking time to listen to him, and honour Rocky's feelings and his personal space boundaries. He spent some more time standing with Rocky at a distance and offering his hand toward Rocky, then withdrawing or retreating if Rocky said No with his body language.

In time, Tom was able to stroke Rocky on the neck, with Rocky feeling more relaxed and accepting on closer proximity and touch. This all took quite a bit of time, for the two to become comfortable in each other's proximity, and find a way to connect, with relaxation, in a way that felt mutually beneficial.

"Not only is the practitioner skilfully holding an I-Thou relationship with both the horse and client, she is demonstrating the core principle of Ethical practice by considering, "Is this good for the horse?""

"This sounds like an important core theme – trying to get attention. There is likely a developmentally significant unmet need for attunement, attention, and being seen, and he has been trying to meet this need (unconsciously or without awareness) as an adult in different, unsuccessful ways (via management strategies/ behaviour patterns). This important theme can be tagged in the therapist's mind, if it is not appropriate to deepen further in the context of the group setting and the broader role, function and therapeutic goals of the specific EAP group."

"This sounds like a very important relationship experiment focused around listening to others, noticing their feelings, boundaries, wants and needs, and finding a way to connect – where it is mutually beneficial. If he could take these new skills to apply to his human relationships, things may start changing in his life. Of course, his core theme around a yearning to be seen and heard, needs to be explored too, in time, for his relationships to fundamentally change."

During integration and closure of that group session, Tom said he was now curious and open to exploring what this might look like with people in his house and in his life. Instead of continuing with behaviour that other's may experience as being annoying and or even rude (ignoring their feelings, wants and requests), Tom wanted to be, in his words "more patient and polite".

When Tom came back to group therapy the following week, he reported that his experimenting had gone really well! The other men in the equine group therapy, who lived with Tom in the house agreed, he had been easier to live with. Tom basked in a moment of experiencing some 'healthy pride' – feeling proud of his capacity to support change in his life and in the lives of others.

The horses, particularly Rocky, offered Tom an incredible opportunity to notice his behaviour, notice how his behaviour might affect others and experiment with different ways of doing things – all with the power of here and now learning. Tom learned through experience, not just thinking about a pattern and thinking about change, but actually *trying something new*, checking it out for himself and with the other (Rocky), to support a new open curiosity and experience of relational change.

> "It is common that participants and clients often go home after an EAP session with some new curiosity and experiment that they are interested in exploring for themselves. This 'homework' transitions the personal development and learning into other life domains, which is essential for longer term change."

SESSION 2

MORE BOUNDARIES

During our second Boundary Session, the men were invited to explore and experiment with having a clear 'No' boundary, standing up for themselves and communicating it to others in their lives. In order to explore this boundary-setting, the men were asked to stand within a hula hoop and ask their horse partner to stay out of the hoop.

Extra guidelines included being able to build a re-lationship with their horse, being able to touch and stroke the horse, but staying firm with their boundary and communications and not stepping out of the hula hoop or allowing the horse to step in.

The guys were given further support about how they might make a request to the horse, to step back if they were approaching, by gently pushing on the horse's nose, or gently moving the lead-rope.

All of my herd can respond to the slightest sugges-tion or request on the body or through the lead-rope, but sometimes they choose not to, depending on the request and the person making the request!

One guy, Mike, who appears in group therapy context, generally, as not very assertive. He talks softly, if at all, and tends to withdraw from social contact. His equine partner was Rumour, who can be quite expressive, forward and comfortable to say, or do, what he wants. Rumour kept stepping into the hoop, Mike kept backing away. I noticed and I asked Mike if he would like some support. Mike said, "No thanks." I gave him some more time to experiment.

As the group process was unfolding, I occasionally offered different ideas and curiosities to the whole group, as I noticed many of the guys were finding the process of communicating boundaries a little difficult.

Eventually, I asked Mike to stop for a moment. He stopped. I inquired into the thoughts that were going through his mind to get a sense of what he was ex-periencing and thinking about. He said he just kept saying, "Please back up Rumour" and was wishing Rumour would just do it. I was starting to get curious about whether this was a tendency or pattern in his life that perhaps people tended to be like Rumour, doing what they wanted around him and not doing what he wanted (or hoped for).

He said, "Yes." I noticed he looked a little sad about acknowledging this. I wondered out loud with Mike about what it would look like if he was clearer with what he wanted and clearer with communicating what he wanted with others? What would it be like for you to be heard?"

He was interested in what this might look like, and how he might experiment with having a voice, being heard and communicating with others in a clear way about what he hoped for or wanted.

We started to brainstorm some possible ways that he could experiment with in expressing himself. I offered him an experiment to experience what it would be like to express himself clearly by opening his shoulders, lengthening his spine and offering himself the thought (in his mind), such as "Rumour, go back."

Clear, direct and communicated through his mind and his body. We brainstormed some other things he could do to experiment with this a little. Mike took an outbreath, put his shoulders back and looked at Rumour. Rumour instantly stopped. Then, after a moment, Rumour continued to move forward.

I offered Mike some extra ideas and after some time Rumour stopped, and then actually stepped back! A small smile came to Mike's lips. At that moment Rumour chose to move forward again. Mike almost gave up but then I watched him stand tall and try again. Once again Rumour stopped and stepped back. The smile returned.

Rumour and Mike played with this communication for some time. Over time, I could see Mike was starting to stand up much taller and straighter. It was a delight to see him experiencing and experimenting in relationship with Rumour, discovering what it was like to be together with someone and to say what he wanted, with strength and clarity.

During the integration and closure part of the group session, Mike shared some of his reflection. "It might feel scary to stick up for your rights, but if you stick at it long enough eventually, they leave you

"Sounds like an important theme – speaking up, having a voice, expressing and communicating to others what he really wants."

alone." There was a long way to go in the exploration of expressing to others what he felt and wanted, but this was a start!

SESSION 3

AND MORE BOUNDARIES!

One of my herd members, Vali, is an Andalusian horse, with a traumatized past. Consequently, he is very fearful around humans. To get close to Vali requires people to be very grounded, very present and quite perceptive to the subtle changes in his body language and overall expression, and communications. To look after his needs as a horse with trauma, I invite him to participate in sessions at liberty - so that he has the freedom to move away when he chooses.

During this session, Andrew decided he wanted to make contact with Vali. Andrew had shared with the group that he had a lot of anger issues, and, that he struggled with controlling it.

During this session, I supported him to make contact with Vali, as he wished, and I encouraged him to use his out-breath, and to keep his nervous system regulated. I also supported Andrew to resource himself with a grounding technique that we often use in equine assisted sessions. This way he would keep noticing his feet on the ground, bringing his focus and attention towards the ground, the earth, rather than up high in his chest or in his head.

Andrew persevered, breathing, grounding, approaching, waiting, and moving away from Vali, for a very long time. Every time Andrew started to get frustrated, I noticed that Vali would quickly step away. I offered some of the observations that I was noticing in him and in Vali.

With my support Andrew started to notice and track all the subtleties of body language, and started

"Such incredibly valuable bio-feedback from Vali the horse. So, clear, so experiential, learning in real relationship. This is one of the most important ways horses can support awareness and growth for clients, learning in relationship."

to pick up on the most subtle changes happening for Vali. The whole group became transfixed watching this very intimate exploration and delicate balance, of Andrew getting too close, moving too quick and Vali moving away. Just as our time was nearly up, Vali lowered his head and allowed Andrew to come in close, so close that Vali sniffed his hand! What a beautiful moment!

In the integration and reflection part of the session, Andrew shared spontaneously that it was the first time he has been able to notice the very beginning sensations of his anger. He shared that, initially he couldn't understand why Vali would move away. Then with time and repetition, gradually noticed that Vali moved as soon as he started to hold his breath!

As Andrew experimented with his breathing, specifically offering himself many out-breaths and regulating himself with his breath, he became aware of a tightness in his shoulders. He realized this was an early sign of his anger. This was such a new awareness and insight! Andrew said he couldn't believe that he could regulate his anger just by breathing, grounding and pausing.

"Wow! What a profound and important new awareness."

It really felt very new and exciting for Andrew to be noticing such important information about his body and his experience, how it impacted him, and his relationship with others. Of course, the group participants benefit from each-others' learning, insight and new awareness, so the change can ripple through many individuals in this way.

"This is an important and unique benefit of group process and group therapy, there can be layers of personal growth and layers of learning that is happening as participants witness and hear each-others process, and have their own response and learning to each-others themes and process."

The following week, in the next group therapy session, Andrew shared that during the previous week he had noticed and tracked his emerging tension, much sooner, and, was able to interrupt the development of his anger by going for a walk before he got really angry or becoming out of control.

This was so exciting to share this development with him, how he was not only tracking how his anger developed in the body, but he was now also able to build quite solid affective regulation skills to safely support and express his anger, ensuring it didn't develop into aggression or 'out of control anger'.

What an accomplishment from that one, session with Vali. Vali's trauma behaviour and hypervigilance supported Andrew's personal growth in a way that was very poignant and beautiful to witness.

SESSION 4

EXPLORING LIFE CHALLENGES

In one of the final group therapy sessions, I invited the group participants to explore any current challenges they may be facing in their lives. I invited them to utilise a selection of the various creative materials provided as props (like coloured hoops, streamers, cones, tubs, etc) and build a representation of a recent challenge they were worrying about.

We call this a projective experiment, where clients are asked to externalise a feeling, part of self, or significant experience (a current challenge), by utilising materials, and then representing it in a physical form on the horse arena. The inner experience (internalised experience of a "recent challenge") then gets externalised, for clients to experience differently, reflect on and learn from.

Importantly, we then offer opportunities for the horses to freely interact with the representation, supporting this creative process (much like live, relational art therapy!), so it is brought to life in the here and now.

Two of the guys, Larry and Connor, were about to become House Leaders due to others moving out of the house into transition accommodation. They were feeling apprehensive about this new change, perceived step up, and increase in responsibilities.

"This is an example of why there is no such thing as a "good" therapy horse or a "trained/ certified" therapy horse. Certifying therapy horses or requiring EAP horses to have a certain temperament, have a certain training, history, and set of behaviours, is not only ignorant about the fundamentals of EAP itself, it is potentially unsafe (for clients).

Some practitioners (untrained and un-certified themselves in EAP or EAL) are unfortunately purchasing and certifying their "therapy horse" without having any training or certification for themselves, as practitioners. This, I believe, is unprofessional, unethical, potentially unsafe and a big concern for the development of the field of animal assisted therapy, equine assisted psychotherapy and equine assisted learning.

Vali's contribution to client change was safe, powerful and relational. The facilitator has 100% responsibility - to know their horses, maintain their horses' safety and welfare, maintain their clients' safety and welfare, and be trained in the modality they are providing (EAP / EAL/ AAT / AAL). It is the Practitioners' responsibility to be trained, acting in accordance within their scope of practice, and making appropriate professional decisions regarding their animals, clients and services."

They began depicting this challenge by using a traffic cone inside a hula hoop (which represented them). Between the two hula hoops they also added another taller cone within a hula hoop, decorated with all sorts of materials such as feathers and ribbons. This taller, decorated cone, they shared with the group, represented what it felt like being a leader and all the fears of believing "maybe I am not good enough to be house leader".

I then invited the herd into the arena at liberty. Straight away, the herd leader, Savvy, went to this creative representation. He pulled all of the materials off the centre cone and threw them off to the side. He then picked up each cone that represented the guys and placed the cones in the middle leadership hula hoop. He then stood beside the 'leadership' cone and appeared to go to sleep. This was something that all of the group members and myself noticed!

During inquiry, I asked what meaning they made of what Savvy had just done with their projective representation. Firstly, they said, "Savvy wrecked it!" We explored this a little, "What was that like?"

The participants then explored some more, with the representation of the fears of not being good enough, and moved the cones (that represented themselves) and put them back into their own hula hoops. At that moment, Savvy opened his eyes, he turned to these cones, picked them up, and replaced them as he had done before! The guys were now looking incredulous.

I asked, "What are you noticing? What does this mean to you?" Larry said, "It's like he thinks we are good enough to be leaders!" Connor agreed, adding, that they have Savvy's' seal of approval.

I inquired about the way Savvy had removed the 'fear' material from the leadership cone. Larry became curious, and said it was like "Savvy was telling me not to be so worried... Savvy thinks we are good enough!" Connor agreed. I asked how they

"It's important to note that part of what the participants appeared to be looking for was reassurance or feedback from others 'you got this'. This is a start. Over time, we hope that clients themselves will be interested in what they believe about themselves, but, sometimes we desire mirroring and recognition from others as adults (i.e. that I am OK, I am enough, I am competent, etc.), especially if we did not get this core attachment need met as children, or, if we developed a pattern of looking outside ourselves for confirmation This is something practitioners would track, notice and perhaps document in case notes, and choose when or if (given the contract) they may address these developmental, core self-organisation patterns."

were feeling about their new roles, after exploring this today with Savvy and the rest of the group. Larry said, "I feel more comfortable actually." Connor said, "I feel a bit happier about it."

PRACTITIONER REFLECTION

I am always fascinated by what the herd brings to these sessions and what it does for the participants. The horses can behave so differently, from one person to the next, and one session to the next. It never ceases to surprise me.

Equine Assisted Psychotherapy practice is so relational, spontaneous, experiential and experimental. It is a delight to never really know what is about to happen and what people might learn with the horses, but to remain openly curious about what is unfolding, and what it could mean in the broader context of peoples' lives.

Chapter 10

CHAQUITA THE SAFE OTHER – ADULT WITH COMPLEX TRAUMA

PRACTITIONER INFORMATION

DEBORAH WALKER is a registered psychologist of 20 years. Clinically she has extensive experience in the treatment of trauma, mood disorders and pain. In her early years as a psychologist, Deborah developed a curiosity about what "treatments work" and for whom, as well as the factors that cause clients to "not benefit from therapy" or stop attending therapy. This curiosity developed into a passion for providing diversity in therapeutic modality. In addition to Cognitive Behavioural Therapy, Solution Focused Psychotherapy, EMDR, ACT, Strategic Psychotherapy, Deborah has also studied Interpersonal Neurobiology with Dr Dan Siegel, the treatment of Depression and Trauma with Dr Michael Yapko, the treatment of trauma through working with the somatic and the nervous system with Peter Levine, Pat Ogden and Bessel Van De Kolk and most powerfully integrating horses into the therapeutic environment with Meg Kirby and Noel Haarburger of The Equine Psychotherapy Institute.

Deborah studies, and experience have led her to, where clinically appropriate, integrate horses and a nature-based environment into psychological interventions and understand the vital importance of experiential learning i.e. not just "talking about it".

THE ENVIRONMENT

Trinity Psychologists operates on the Sunshine Coast on a beautiful 10 acre property, 15 mins from the coast. Deb cares for a herd of six horses, 5 chickens and 3 dogs, all whom seem to find a way of safely including themselves in psychology sessions! Deborah's husband Noel is also a psychologist and is also trained in Equine Assisted Psychotherapy through the Institute.

CLIENT INFORMATION

PLEASE NOTE: *the language used in this chapter includes non-gender specific pronouns of they, their and them and OM is a pseudonym for the client.*

OM is mid-40s. OM was seeking help with the sequlea of complex trauma and had decided to try therapy again after what was described as "a number of failed attempts" at room-based therapy of various forms. OM explained that the previous experience of counselling, especially talking about the painful things that had happened, had caused a frightening re-emergence of the use of alcohol and drugs to block out memories and this had caused great detriment to OM's social and occupational functioning.

OM reported a deep sense of feeling broken and empty, terror at the thought of "opening up again", fear of being judged and rejected, feeling "wired" and having a sense of being unsafe all the time and most importantly for OM not having any connection with themselves or anyone else. OM said at sometime in early life they had become lost. OM reported a sense of running out of time for any sense of meaning in life.

OM explained that they had found out from a friend that I provided the option of working outdoors, with horses. OM also had a clear memory of being young and being with horses, and feeling safe. So, on this basis OM thought "it was worth another go" (psychological and psychotherapy work) especially if they could have access to working outside in nature, with horses.

"This is an unfortunate reality for many clients whom have experienced psychological support with practitioners who are not trauma-informed in their practice, as the narrative based work, telling stories, allowing or requiring clients to re-tell their history without a trauma-informed approach can sometimes lead to unintentional harm and reinforce the clients' experience of being dysregulated and unable to manage their experience, feelings and trauma memories."

REASON FOR WORKING WITH HORSES

As OM had experienced difficulties with traditional room based CBT and had a clear interest in a setting that included horses and the outdoors, it seemed

CHAQUITA THE SAFE OTHER – ADULT WITH COMPLEX TRAUMA

appropriate to trial an alternative setting (including EPI model equine assisted interventions) supporting OM to explore meaningful change.

The EPI Model integrates - trauma-informed practice (working with resourcing, regulating and soothing the clients' nervous system, and reprocessing trauma, within the client's window of tolerance); addresses relationship and attachment disturbance (via working within the I-Thou therapeutic relationship with practitioner and horses); and works with awareness and mindfulness (including sensory, somatic, emotional, cognitive and behavioural awareness), all safely developing the ability for *psychological safety, choice and healthy expression*. This deeply relational, trauma-informed, attachment-focused and awareness-based approach with animals in a natural setting, appeared to be a clinical best-fit for OM, given their trauma presentation and history.

"Resourcing, regulating, relationship and awareness are all core principles of the AWARE TherapyTM approach."

THERAPEUTIC GOALS

OM's overall therapeutic goals were:

• to create a connection with themselves and others

• to connect to self-experience, express and make requests

• express themselves without fear

• to feel good about themself

• to tolerate strong emotion without the need for numbing out

"It is essential that practitioners assess and consider exactly why they choose the psychological interventions and psychotherapeutic environment that they do with each client to ensure "best practice". Equine assisted psychotherapy is not a one-size fits all approach to psychotherapy and psychological intervention, as the clinical reasoning for the what and how of practice must be supported and documented to ensure it meets the high professional standards and ethics of the allied health discipline utilised."

ORIENTING INFORMATION

Right from the start we worked on stage one trauma work, so we could then move onto stage two trauma work and process traumatic memories and fixed patterns. We focused on - building OM's ability to resource and self-regulate, both in session and im-

"At the Institute we teach a 3 Stage Model of Trauma Resolution, including -

1. Building safety, support, stabilisation and symptom reduction

2. Renegotiating traumatic memories

3. Integration and meaning making"

portantly out of session; building OM's capacity to experience and create pleasant experiences, in the here and now; helping OM know and express their no and yes through boundary work; and building OM's capacity to experience and tolerate (within their window of tolerance) uncomfortable sensations and feelings; addressing and reprocessing the traumatic history and the unhelpful fixed beliefs and behaviours.

CHECK IN/ASSESSMENT/ CONTRACTING

At the previous session we had agreed to work on experimenting with making requests as OM has difficulty identifying what they want and then expressing this. OM arrived at the session in an agitated state. OM described themselves as feeling extremely fidgety and wanting to move and this was congruent with the practitioner's observations of OM's body language, language and posture. We agreed that we would go out into the herd and Deborah was comfortable with OM's ability to be safe, aware and set appropriate boundaries within the herd. Prior to going out into the herd we brought ourselves into the here and now with awareness and resourcing exercises, and the safety guidelines, to re-establish OM's focus on safety.

EQUINE EXPERIENCES

I invited OM to meet and move with the herd with their agitation in a safe way. We explored OM's experience of wanting to move, and through *mindful movement* we noticed how OM's sense of agitation changed over time. We also explored moving in ways that mirrored the herd's movement, with a mindful use of breath and body.

"This is a nice summary of some of the essential psychological and self-regulation skills that trauma clients must develop to start to move out of a dysregulated state (whether sympathetic nervous or dorsal vagal nervous state) and into a regulated state (ventral vagal state of connection or rest and digest, as The Polyvagal theory describes, Stephen Porges)."

"This appeared to be an important clinical choice-point, to be able to offer the client the opportunity (given the presenting state of agitation and activation of the nervous system in what appears to be a sympathetic arousal state) to move, walk and allow the body to mobilise and express through movement."

"Very important to continually assess and support the clients' capacity to touch into regulation and the ventral vagal state, perhaps with a "ventral brake" moment, as Deb Dana so eloquently describes, bringing "a little ventral to the sympathetic state" (Deb Dana's video series "An Introduction to Applying Polyvagal Therapy in Clinical Practice")."

"This slowing down and bringing mindfulness to the movement, and the moving in connection with the horses or herd, gives not just the nervous system a chance to regulate, but allows a heightening of awareness for the client in a safe and titrated way, as the awareness is happening inside the container of other relational and physiological resources (including being resourced and supported by the presence of the practitioner, the presence and movement of the horses, and, the natural environment)."

OM shared feeling more and more grounded, and yet also having particular sensations in OM's body that were arising. We began to explore OM's experience with the sensations. Just at this time, one of the older mares that OM had worked with previously (Chaquita) came and stood close to OM, occasionally nudging OM. OM said they felt supported by Chaquita's presence, and said "I am not in this alone". OM went on to share the impression or meaning associated with Chaquita's presence and touch. "Chaquita feels her body sensations *all the time* so maybe I can too". This appeared to give OM some support and insight in the moment, and, some confidence to allow them to stay with self-experience and not view the sensations or feelings (i.e. agitation) as a problem.

OM shared a feeling of "hollow, sludgy emptiness" in their belly and a "throbbing, tight, hot feeling" in the throat. We explored these sensations slowly, in some depth. This was certainly something OM had never done before. OM shared their tendency was to usually "shove away" or "numb out" to any uncomfortable sensations. However, in the steady presence of Chaquita and myself, OM was able to stay with, tolerate and explore much further than ever before! We spent time feeling into the experience of emptiness and tightness, and as a support to stay with and not go away or numb out, OM reached out to touch Chaquita's neck. Both Chaquita's presence, and the touch sensations appeared to support OM to be with self-experience in a very new way.

OM noticed both fear and sadness (in the stomach area as well as the throat). The three of us, OM, Chaquita and myself stayed quietly together in an intimate and safe relationship, supporting OM to allow their feelings and inquire into what their feelings might be informing them, about themselves or life. OM said without hesitation "I want to be recognised for who I am and heard". When OM said that Chaquita took a huge outbreath. We spent a few

"The horse-client relationship appeared to facilitate some insight, experience of relational safety, modelling (of an embodied way of life), and resourcing, functioning as a doorway to mindfulness or awareness (which, of course, is inherently disturbing!). The horse-client relationship appeared to foster a new capacity for embodiment and awareness."

"In our EPI model work we can support our clients to notice what the experience or feelings are here to inform the person about, what might want some attention, understanding, regulation, expression and opportunity for completion (from a gestalt therapy perspective allowing the client to attend to unfinished business, into processing and integrating un-processed feelings, needs and memories)."

moments settling into the importance of what OM had just said, and, the unique and important support, that Chaquita had offered.

After a little time, I then asked OM what OM wanted to do. Again, without hesitation, OM expressed "I want to walk with Chaquita and *talk with her*". So, together we found a halter and lead rope, I invited OM to check with Chaquita if she was OK with being haltered. Chaquita gave her consent (it appeared) by moving her nose towards OM and the halter, with a soft expression in her eyes.

OM and Chaquita then spent about ten minutes walking together, with OM speaking out loud to her. OM expressed a desire to do this without my presence, and I had agreed, given I know Chaquita very well and she is a mare who has a history of walking safely with a diverse range of people, additionally, I was tracking Chaquita's body language and her relaxed nervous system and behaviour. I remained close by, observing, with softness through my body and presence, allowing the two beings to be in a relationship, in a safe, intimate and unique way, determined by their-selves. Chaquita walked with OM, matching OM's footsteps. She kept an ear on OM the whole time and at times turned her face and neck towards OM. The connection between them was a delight to witness. I noticed my joy and regulated nervous system, observing and holding space from a safe distance to support their very intimate process.

REFLECTION

This trauma informed and relational approach to therapy that the horses (and Chaquita, particularly) and myself provided, supported a careful exploration of somatic awareness, emotional awareness, and expression. All of this was, in previous sessions, outside of OM's ability and window of tolerance. By

"The practitioner-client-horse therapeutic triad appeared to be a very important part of client process and access to the clients' experience and un-processed psychological material (from the clients' history), perhaps by providing emotional safety, trust, co-regulation, resourcing and a relational container of awareness."

"This is an essential part of the EPI model approach from an ethical and practice methodology perspective - looking for consent from the horse, and including the horses' subjective experience in the session. Thus, it becomes a 'relational experience' that does not unintentionally model violation of ones' feeling and needs in the service of the others' (clients') feelings and needs."

"Beautiful! Great ongoing clinical assessment and intervention, and practitioner self-support — to ensure the session is a 'client-focused' session."

being with Chaquita, OM was able to stay with self-experience, relational experience well within their window of tolerance. The opportunity to integrate and more deeply understand the feelings of agitation, fear and sadness, now became possible! What a unique and wonderful opportunity for OM. In the being together and walking together, OM was able to share *what had previously been unsafe* and *previously been unspoken*. Chaquita was able to provide a corrective experience of being heard and recognised.

In further discussion together, OM shared what it was like to be that expressive of OM's deepest needs and feelings, in relationship with Chaquita. OM stated that they had *never really felt able, supported or un-judged in this way* and in expressing themselves in this way, OM felt a deep sense of "freeness", a sense of "rightness within themself", and a "great sense of relief and ability to breath throughout their body". OM said they had a new sense of being.

It was a deeply emotional experience for me to see the close connection and support Chaquita gave to OM, and the new awareness and insight OM now experienced.

"Yes, this is the therapeutic value for OM, experiencing being safe (when previously experiencing unsafety) and experiencing expressing feelings and needs (when previously OM's feelings and needs were unspoken). What an important and life-changing, corrective experience that both Chaquita and Deborah offered OM in this session."

INTEGRATION

Before leaving the session, OM said "I can ask to be recognised and heard and I felt recognised and heard today without any judgement. I never believed that would be possible without a great deal of pain".

"I also feel a huge relief and sense of peace in my body when I did this. I don't need to avoid these feelings anymore. And I have learnt that with support and in relationship I can tolerate these feelings and most importantly I can stay with myself and express my needs".

Again it was clear from my observations of OM's nervous system, and body language that OM was indeed experiencing themselves in a very new, calmer, more integrated way.

AFTERNOTE

As a choicepoint, I could have asked OM to tell me what she expressed privately with Chaquita, however, I knew the horses especially Chaquita would provide the safe and needed relational holding for OM. I trusted Chaquita and their connection. That felt important at the time.

We have gone on (in subsequent sessions) to speak the unspeakable and OM has gone on to experience themselves in a new and expressive way and is getting to know themselves in a powerful and life-giving way.

"

"I-Thou Horse-person-ship has as its primary focus, regard for the horse, his or her feelings, wants and needs, as the most important intention in the relationship."

MEG KIRBY

Chapter 11

LILY AND THE SPACIOUS HERD – ADOLESCENT PERSONAL DEVELOPMENT SESSION

PRACTITIONER INFORMATION

PAULA JEWELL is an Equine Assisted Learning Practitioner, student of Counselling and Psychology and Program Manager at The Equine Psychotherapy Institute. After a career in human services, specialising in homelessness and family violence, Paula then transitioned into the world of farmed animal rescue, spending 9 years at Edgar's Mission farmed animal sanctuary. This trajectory brought Paula up close and personal with the innate wisdom of animals and developed her appreciation for the individual life and story of every human and animal she encounters. Paula's own healing journey has fuelled her passion to empower others, particularly children and young females, to build healthy relationships with themselves, their bodies and emotions to live full and enriching lives.

Paula is the owner of Macedon Ranges Animal Assisted Learning, and manages an animal sanctuary named Sunshine Hill, with her husband Darin, where she focuses on rehabilitating chickens in need and incorporating their Wisdom into the EPI Model. Paula, Darin and their feathered friends (all of whom have names and unique personalities) share their lives with Wallace and Dini the dogs, Lily, Bert and Celia the cats, Goldie and Cricket Duckworth the ducks, and Charlie and Ruby the horses.

CLIENT BACKGROUND

PLEASE NOTE: *Melinda is a pseudonym for the client*

Melinda is 15 years of age, currently living at home with both parents and four younger brothers. At the time of the session, Melinda and her brothers had been home schooling for a number of months due to Coronavirus restrictions. Both parents were also working from home. Melinda attended the equine assisted learning session with a curiosity to meet horses, try something new, and learn about herself.

SESSION

I had prepared for Melinda's EAL session and considered working with Stormy who might be a good fit for a new client with no previous experience with horses. Stormy is an older and well-trained mare particularly suited to younger clients. I had mentally prepared to offer Melinda a session from the EPI Horse Wisdom Program, a psycho-educationally based program designed to develop social and emotional skills with targeted learning areas. Given Melinda attended the session without any specific focus areas or learning goals, I came prepared to explore any current challenges she was facing in her life, especially given the context of home schooling, the impact of the Coronavirus, and being unable to connect with friends.

Melinda and I took our chairs and sat, side by side in the sun, overlooking the large hilly paddock where the herd was grazing. Whilst walking to this area, Melinda and I casually checked in and discussed what she had been up to in the days and weeks previously. I had shared a video with Melinda and her mum outlining what Equine Assisted Learning was and asked Melinda if she had had a chance to watch it or had any questions about what we might be doing.

Melinda shared that she had tried to watch it but it was difficult in her household with lots of noise and activity from her younger siblings. I internally noted this response, as a possible emerging theme, as we settled side by side in our chairs to begin the session.

I invited Melinda to tune into her five senses and resource herself. Melinda shared that the vivid green and expanse of the hills was soothing her. She shared that the sense of space brought a feeling of calm to her and that she experienced this within her stomach as a settled sensation. Melinda shared that the openness of the hills was unlike the environment she was used to.

During this part of the session, I noticed Stormy was standing at the gate of the arena, looking toward the hills, where the remainder of the herd was grazing. Stormy was not showing any signs of distress, such as calling out to her herd or pacing the fence line, however, I felt there was a choice point for me as a practitioner. I was internally wondering whether to continue with my planned Horse Wisdom session in the arena or *be guided by both my client's and Stormy's focus upon the hills and the remainder of the herd.*

After offering Melinda the Safety Guideline to support her safety for the session with the horses, I shared with her that I noticed her focus was on the hill, and that I also noticed Stormy gazing out at the same area. I suggested that instead of staying in the arena space with Stormy, perhaps we could let Stormy back out with her friends. Melinda seemed interested in this idea. I then led Stormy as Melinda walked beside us out into the main paddock where we thanked Stormy and I took off her halter. Stormy walked slowly off, towards her herd grazing on the hill.

Melinda and I then stood at the base of the hill looking up at the herd grazing all the way at the top of the hill. I had been sitting up there before Melinda arrived (resourcing myself before the session began) and the herd had appeared very settled, with minimal movement or interaction with me or one another. Combined with the cloudless blue sky, the minimal breeze and the time of day, I felt the conditions made

"So, the practitioner had already tagged a potential emerging theme around "household of noise and activity" impacting Melinda, however, decided to orient towards building awareness and resourcing the client before exploring this potential theme. This is an example of a choice-point! There are always so many, forks in the road (if you like) and decisions about assessment and interventions, that shape the session."

"Another theme emerging here "a sense of space" in the green, the hills and the difference between this, and her home environment. Also the sense of space linked to a 'feeling of settled.' "

"The practitioner choice-point emerging here was to stay in the arena with the planned horse wisdom session or follow the direction of the gaze (of Melinda and Stormy) to the hills and the 'space.' "

"This is where the practitioner shares the choicepoint with the client (who can then influence the direction of the session) with interest, disinterest or some response. Transparency is an important part of our work, as it supports client consent and the invitational nature of the EPI model. The practitioner is following, tracking and trusting the unfolding themes, which requires a strong knowledge of one's underpinning theory of change and practice methodology, to then lean into 'not knowing' what is going to happen next. It preferences trust of the client, the horses, the process, rather than clinging to (outdated) structure, formula or agenda. In the EPI model, it is the practitioners' understanding of the theory of change and the process that drives client-centred practice, rather than any "activities" or "planned structure" (which of course can lead to practitioner-driven practice, out of step with the clients' needs)."

the experiment I was about to offer safe for the herd and my client.

From where we stood at the base of the hill, I offered Melinda an invitation to walk to the top of the hill and observe the herd, paying attention to those she was drawn to and those she wasn't. Given the environment and the age of my client, I told Melinda I would walk alongside her up to the top of the hill. Melinda shared that she felt pleased with this idea!

As we walked, Melinda commented on the feeling of space the hill provided and several times stopped to look around at the view over the neighbouring paddocks and countryside below. I felt this was important for Melinda who appeared to visibly relax, shoulders dropping and speech slowing, the higher we got up the hill. I decided not to interrupt this process for Melinda and stopped and looked around alongside her, without any discussion or inquiry. The space felt important.

As Melinda approached the herd, she shared that she felt safe with the horses because they were each, "just doing their own thing." I asked Melinda to expand upon this a little more to which she shared that the horses knew she was there but that they were content *just being themselves and this helped her feel relaxed.* I asked Melinda what the horses *being themselves* offered her. She shared that it gave her space to be herself too. I smiled, and we breathed out together, in this shared space and shared moment. At this point Melinda paused and observed River, an older Anglo Arabian gelding and I moved a little off to the side, to allow her space to do so. River and Melinda greeted each other, with a sniff, a touch of nose and hand and some time and space.

After this meeting and exchange between River and Melinda, we then sat at the top of the hill for several more minutes. I noticed Melinda was watching the herd but was also looking out at the view below and around her. Again, I felt it was important for Melinda to experience this sense of space and although I wanted

"It is very useful to note how the impact and effectiveness of the EAL session is well under-way, with the clients' nervous system already re-regulating in the green surrounds, the movement, the practitioner presence and skills, the distant presence of the herd, and persistent orienting to the clients' emerging figures of interest and draw towards 'space.' "

"Now we are hearing more about the experience and meaning of "space", as it also includes space for the client 'to be herself.' "

to inquire into what it meant for her, I bracketed this urge and remained quiet whilst she did so.

After some time, I asked Melinda if she would like to meet some of the horses (with me nearby to support her safety). Melinda said yes, she would, so together we moved between the herd members. Melinda approached each horse slowly, with hand outstretched, asking them if they would like to meet her and saying, "That's okay, you enjoy your grass," to those horses who returned to grazing after a brief sniff. I shared with Melinda that I noticed she mentioned the horses' needs often and she replied that it was important to her to give them space to do what they wanted.

At this point Melinda was interacting with stock-horse mare Lexi when Jensen, an 8-year-old Friesian gelding approached her. Melinda again held out her hand to Jensen who, instead of pausing and sniffing as the other herd members had done, continued walking right up to Melinda until he was only centimetres from her face.

Melinda patted Jensen on his neck and he then turned his head in the other direction, put his ears back at Lexi who moved away. He then turned back to Melinda and I heard her say, "Oh gosh you scared me!" and she took a step away. I was next to Melinda and asked her if this felt ok and she said, "Yes, he's just very big and he didn't give me much space."

I shared with Melinda that I noticed she stepped away from Jensen when he got close to her and she replied that she felt like she needed to in order to keep her personal space. I commented that this sounded like a healthy boundary, supporting her safety and her choice. Melinda smiled and agreed that her need to protect her personal space boundaries was important. Jensen moved quietly away.

"Another part of the emerging theme of "space" is now also expanding to include her boundaries and capacity to communicate boundaries with others."

We stood in this place for a moment before I invited Melinda to an area at the top of the hill away from the horses. Once there, I asked a little more about what she was experiencing. Melinda shared again that the horses seemed happy just doing their own thing and it was important to her to give them their space. I asked Melinda if this was something that was important to her too and she said that yes, sometimes she just needed mental and physical space to be able to deal with her day.

Melinda shared that she had a classmate who she felt invaded her emotional space when she shared too many things and Melinda became overwhelmed. She said she sometimes had to move away from her and we again discussed this being a healthy boundary. I mentioned a little about how horses communicate their boundaries, like Jensen had done with Lexi earlier (when he put his ears back and she moved away), and how I had noticed they both returned to grazing after the adjustment of their personal space boundaries.

Melinda shared, and we further discussed, how Jensen the big black horse, had mirrored these big feelings Melinda's classmate triggered in her (when he moved too close to her). We both talked a bit more about how she had kept herself safe with Jensen and listened to her personal space boundary needs. Melinda was particularly interested in how her experience with Jensen felt similar to her experience with her classmate.

Together we did some breathing and grounding on the hill, and afterwards talked about how she could use these techniques to support herself at any time in her life.

Lily, a black, brown and white tobiano Quarter horse cross Arabian mare then approached us. I chose to share with Melinda that in my experience (practitioner self-disclosure) Lily usually hung back during sessions and even walked away if people approached her, so I was a little curious about her approach. Lily sniffed Melinda's face. Melinda and Lily spent a moment together sharing breath and connecting. After some time, Melinda shared, "I think she (Lily) feels safe ... because she knows I'm respecting her space."

"This is a nice link between what is showing up in the themes with the horses and in the EAL session, and in life – at home and school. Sometimes practitioners can inquire into these links, to further explore and integrate the learnings, and other times, it can be noted (by the practitioner) but unspoken in the session. It is a matter of assessment, timing, clients' window of tolerance, developmental age and stage and many other considerations."

Lily interacted with Melinda and stayed in close proximity for quite some time. Melinda and I continued to share together about the concept of personal space. Melinda shared that it felt different when Lily was interacting with her. She felt like Lily "was asking and not demanding" like Jensen had, and she reflected that it didn't feel overwhelming for her, *to be close with Lily.*

INTEGRATION

Melinda had already done quite a lot of processing on the themes of boundaries and space during the session. Toward the end of the session, Melinda shared how life during Coronavirus restrictions had been different for her. She shared that in the mornings on the way to school and on the way home she used to have 10 minutes to herself on the bus, during which she used to just think, gather her thoughts or plan the day ahead. Melinda shared that she didn't realise how important this "mental space" was for her until she didn't have it anymore.

I asked Melinda if there was a way she might be able to incorporate this mental space into her daily life (perhaps as she had done today with the horses) and we discussed strategies such as sitting outside on the deck in the morning, waking up and taking ten minutes before leaving her room to breathe and have space, or finding a quiet spot in the house to pause or even to read. We also discussed ways Melinda could communicate her need for more space with her family. Melinda had lots of ideas about how she could integrate her learning from today's experience with the horses into her life.

Melinda talked about her yoga class and how she appreciated being around people during the class, especially when they had their "own mental bubble", as this gave her a feeling of space. Melinda shared that she hadn't realised how important this was to her and that she would continue to find ways to give herself this space.

"Here, Melinda had a chance to further explore how it feels to experience contact with another, that feels mutually agreeable, incudes listening to each party, rather than one party demanding or forcing or violating the other with their needs or wants dominating. Through Lily, Melinda could also put into words, her own wants, wishes and boundaries. Here, the horse contributes to client change by - modelling negotiating boundaries, modelling healthy relationship, potentially being a projective mechanism for deeper insight, potentially offering safe and authentic relationship in the here and now, evoking a feeling experience of joy, safety and trust, amongst many other possibilities."

"This is another dimension of the emergent theme of "space" as now the client is also exploring "mental space" and what that means to her, feels like and does for her, in her life."

"The integration stage in EAL is often very fruitful, as we get to explore more about how the learning, insight, awareness and curiosity that emerged in the session can be applied in life – at home, school, work and other life domains. Here Melinda was able to share more about her needs and wants and was supported by the practitioner to intentionally orient to meeting her own needs via paying attention and bringing the spirit of experimenting back into home life! This is where a lot of the value and effectiveness of EAP and EAL can impact clients, as they transition out of the safety of the session environment, back into life, with change that lasts."

We then took a moment to pause, thank the horses, and walked down the hill together, with a quiet smile on both of our faces.

PRACTITIONER REFLECTION

As a relatively new practitioner, I am still learning to trust the process of EAL and to remember there is immense beauty and potentially profound wisdom to be found in simplicity. Although it is important for me in these early stages of my career to prepare sessions ahead of time, this particular session reminded me to be flexible, drawing on the guidance provided by the model, the client, the horses, and the environment, to shape the experiment that is needed in any moment.

I realise had I been attached to my plans in the beginning of the session (internally) a very different experience would have emerged for the client. This session reminded me how important it is to pay attention to and be guided by the horses and their wisdom as well as the natural world, in order for what is true for a client to emerge. For me, this is where the true transformative potential of this work lies!

I was astounded and inspired by my client's intelligent and intuitive reflection during what on the surface appeared to be an incredibly simple experiment. Again, I reflect that it is important for me to not get hijacked by the need for an EAL session to be about 'doing' but often about 'being'. In this particular session, the horses modelled 'being' perfectly and enabled Melinda to do the same.

In every session, I learn something new about life from the horses alongside whom we work, and I am endlessly honoured to share their innate wisdom and teachings with others.

"This is just one example of the AWARE Therapy™ principle of the Wisdom Approach – appreciating and drawing upon the innate wisdom of horses, animals and the natural world is a core component of this work and brings aliveness and an incredible capacity for growth to each session and client."

" *Horses see the real you. Being seen is incredibly healing.* "

MEG KIRBY

Chapter 12
CALM AND STEADY LEWIS – ADOLESCENT WITH COMPLEX TRAUMA

PRACTITIONER
INFORMATION

NADINE is a Mental Health Social Worker working in the Hunter Valley, NSW. Nadine specialises in working with children and adolescents with complex needs, including autism, range of intellectual capacity, and diverse clinical diagnoses and presentations.

Nadine is the Director of Hunter Valley Children's Therapies, which is a full time equine assisted psychotherapy business, providing services to young people across the beautiful Hunter Valley district and beyond.

Hunter Valley Children's Therapies is always full, and maintains a wait list, as the services are much needed in the community and in high demand. Nadine relishes the opportunity to support young people to develop essential life skills, providing an environment that facilitates full expression of the unique children who she works with, ensuring they experience a safe relational container to reach towards their potential.

CLIENT INFORMATION

PLEASE NOTE: *Alicia is a pseudonym for the client*

Alicia is 14 years of age and diagnosed with Post Traumatic Stress Disorder. Alicia has a history of abuse, neglect, and abandonment by her biological mother whom had a significant substance addiction. Alicia is living with her Nan (maternal grandmother), and they have formed a strong bond. Alicia struggles with suicidality.

Alicia has been attending EAP for approximately a year and broad therapeutic goals include - to experience safety, trust and continuity in relationship, to support the client to regulate her own nervous system when she becomes triggered and dysregulated, and to continue to develop social, emotional, somatic skills to negotiate life, relationships and the stresses of everyday life without falling back into suicidal ideation.

ORIENTING TO THE SESSION

In the previous session, Alicia had requested for her psychologist Michael to attend an equine session, and for us to explore some themes around safety. This seemed like a wonderful plan, given our overall therapeutic goals about safety in relationship!

When Alicia arrived, she was pleasantly surprised that her Psychologist, Michael, was already here. Michael hadn't seen her for a couple of months and he commented on how relaxed she looked. Alicia was excited to introduce him to each of the horses and explained to him some of the 'Horse Wisdom' she had learnt so far in sessions, in particular, how to read their body language to see how they were feeling. Alicia also explained to Michael that "Lewis does big outbreaths" and this reminds her to breathe.

"This collaborative work between EAP and other allied health practitioners in clients' lives can be very supportive (when it's the clients' idea), to foster 'safe people' and 'safe relationships' and a network, particularly for young people who have historically been suicidal and need intensive support at times."

"What a lovely opportunity for the client to be the 'expert', step into agency and educate the carers."

150

Being a herd animal and a prey animal, horses are attuned to those around them. When we connect with horses and share space, the process of neuroception means that they can sense dysregulation, either in themselves or those around them and will attempt to re-regulate with behaviours such as breathing out, yawning, shaking, blowing their nose or licking and chewing with their mouth. These behaviours discharge their nervous system. They will often do these behaviours when they sense either their own 'activation' or that of those around them and it helps them return to a feeling of calm or 'regulation'.

Alicia mentioned to Michael and myself that she had a confrontation with a young person at school earlier today. She had been told by a female student that this male student had called her a 'slut'. She confronted him about it, he neither confirmed nor denied it, and she pushed him. She was able to explore how he might have felt in that moment, when she walked up to him in an intimidating manner and how he may not have been able to think of an answer right away (Michael pointed out how his brain might have not been able to work efficiently while he was feeling intimidated by her). Alicia seemed open to these ideas, and was listening.

We moved over to the arena, where there is a lot of materials around the side of the arena, and I invited Alicia "*to use the materials here and build something that represents your feelings of safety.*"

Alicia struggled a little with where to begin with this representation and how to build it. I wondered whether the experiment and creative concept of building a representation of safety was a little abstract for her. So, I allowed a little time for her to soak on it and then gave some prompts and ideas, to help her to make a start and see what happened! A little bit of support and away she went!

She shared that being with "Nan", is where she feels most safe. Alicia shared that Nan has always been there

"Sounds like both practitioners moved towards more of a psycho-educational approach here, as a choice-point. This is a valid choice. A psychotherapy choice point here would have been to follow and track the experience of pushing the boy, the feelings that emerged, the thoughts that emerged, the meaning and perhaps what the pushing 'did' for her (linked to her history or family of origin themes, and perhaps her anger about feeling unseen, un-cared for, abandoned etc)."

for her and described some situations from her child-hood where Nan had taken her to her house (when she was younger and lived with her mother) and she had cared for her, when her mother couldn't.

Alicia built this representation for Nan. She had a barrel for Nan's body, with a witch's hat for the head and some pool noodles as arms. She also had a shovel for her 'weapon' to protect herself. She commented that Nan always had lots of gardening tools that she could have used to protect herself. She said that she had never had to use these though. She drew a picture on the witch's hat of Nan, the shovel, the pitch-fork and a knife.

We then asked her to identify what the opposite of 'safe' was for her. She used the word 'unsafe' and we invited her to build a representation for this. She explained that there was a house in her old town that came to mind as her 'unsafe' place. She had lots of traumatic memories related to this house. She used some wood to build a representation for this house and spray painted it with brown on the walls and blue on the roof – like the house was. She added the feelings of 'anger' and 'fear' to the house. This creation was significantly physically smaller than the other one, however created a lot more emotional disturbance for her.

"Linked to the 'psychotherapy themes' mentioned above about the anger or rage carried (potentially) from abuse and neglect in infancy childhood, may also have been explored here in the context of needing "a weapon" to protect herself. Again the (potentially) unexplored anger or rage and fear or panic from the past may want some more attention, given the need for weapons to protect from danger (or a lack of safety in the environment). Nan is the safety, the safe place, but she still needs weapons."

"This is an opportunity now for the anger and fear to be named and explored, with this second projective experiment."

Michael and I shared our observations of her body language and tone of voice when she spoke of and stood near her safe and then unsafe spaces. Alicia was interested to hear. While she was in the area of her safe space, she was smiling, standing up tall, her shoulders were back and she spoke in a jovial tone.

When in her 'unsafe' space, her shoulders were slouched, she was looking to the ground and spoke in a softer tone. She was surprised to learn that her body language (and nervous state) had changed so much and that we could notice it.

Alicia was also really keen to have a mounted experience with her favourite horse, Lewis. She asked for this, and both Michael and I felt there was enough time left in the session and that it was a good potential way to further explore the emerging themes and then integrate and close the session.

I offered for her to halter Lewis and bring him out of the paddock. Her initial response was, "I can't put the halter on." I suggested she try some different, more supportive thoughts, like "I can try" (as an experiment) and see what happened. She tried again and this time, put his halter on.

As I invited, supported and prepared the horse for her to sit on his back, she explained that she was feeling nervous. I suggested she take some outbreaths, as she took the three steps up onto the mounting block. Once at the top, she said she was still feeling nervous. I asked about her somatic experience of that. Alicia shared the feeling was in her stomach and it was telling her that she was scared. I asked what she does (at other times) to support herself when she's scared and she suggested music and singing. So, we supported her to try singing! She was nervous about doing that in front of us, so she asked us to face the opposite direction, which we happily agreed. While standing on the top step of the mounting block, Alicia sang a fabulous song, keeping

"I am imagining that the practitioner has something in mind to further explore the themes...whilst mounted and supported by the horse (Lewis)."

"A new experiment to bring into the session, which arrived from the clients' sharing that music and singing is a way she resources herself to release, express and perhaps re-regulate her nervous system."

the beat by clapping with her hands. It was quite a powerful experience for me to watch her standing up high and singing in such a beautiful and empowered way. Once she finished, she said she felt better and ready to hop on the horse (the horse still appeared to remain regulated throughout the entire song!).

Once mounted, she said she could feel her heart racing. To support her interest in her own experience, I offered for her to wear my watch which can track her heart rate. Once she had it on, her HR was around 107 BPM. I shared a little about how our heart rate can increase for different reasons. One being, if we increase our physical activity or movement, our heart needs to pump more blood around our body. Another cause can be triggered from our thoughts. Particularly, how our brain (after receiving the thoughts) can tell our body that there is cause for concern, and so our heart beats faster in preparation for 'fight' or 'flight'. Alicia quietly listened, and, appeared to settle in a few moments.

Once settled, I asked Alicia if she felt OK moving into a walk and perhaps exploring her safe place, from the back of the horse. She said she would definitely like to do that! We walked together, and we noticed the different parts of her representations, with Alicia from horse back! As we approached the representations, I invited Alicia to share what she was experiencing (and specifically feeling somatically). She put some words to her body experience and feeling experience as she approached the safe place.

Earlier in the session, she had told us that she had previously been with a carer who had done a lot of running. They used to run through the bush together and had yell-out out a phrase, "I own the jungle." It seemed that this had been an empowering experience for her. So, I invited Alicia to try yelling this out, here today! (to see what happens). She had been a little hesitant at first, but then appeared to enjoy yelling from the back of the horse (and Lewis seemed to remain regulated and OK with this noise).

"Another expression experiment, to support the client to safely move into expression rather than avoid or hold her feelings in or back. Safe expression can also allow the nervous system to release excess energy and disturbance in the body and hence re-regulate. Given it worked so well in the first verbal experiment, looks like an effective support for this client, with some elements of lightness and play too."

Alicia had an opportunity to offer herself some words of encouragement "I own this place", which appeared to have a great impact, soothing her nervous system and creating some more positive self-talk, to engage her thoughts and mind.

We then moved towards exploring her representation of the 'unsafe' place. Alicia had quite a significant physical response. We walked over slowly and as we got closer, she became more and more disturbed. She said she felt fearful. At one point, her heartrate had increased to 156BPM by just standing near this object. Her physical responses indicated to me a body-based trauma response to those experiences. I used some techniques of pendulation to support her to turn towards, and return to, the safe place. Once there, her BPM lowered, and in good time we returned to the unsafe place. We repeated this moving between the safe place and the unsafe place, again and again, ensuring she was staying well inside her window of tolerance, as well as enlisting her agency (in directing us), and overtime her BPM returned to a stable place.

Along the way, the horse Lewis self-regulated in different ways. He yawned, blew his nose, shook his neck and did lots of outbreaths. Each time, I suggested to Alicia that she offer herself an outbreath to help calm herself, based on the horse's feedback. Given the timing of each of these behaviours from the horse, it certainly seemed as though he was sensing tension and disturbance in her nervous system and making attempts to shift that energy and stress, back to a regulated state.

Horses live in the present moment; they are alert and aware and present to their somatic experience. They sense changes in the field (Alicia, ourselves, the broader environment) and changes in their inner field (in their body) and they utilise immediate release, expression or responsive behaviours, in an attempt to re-regulate their nervous system or calm or regulate those in the immediate proximity. I will often share

"Luckily, the client had the support of externalisation (the projection / representation of unsafe place) and co-regulation (of Lewis' movement, holding, presence, and both practitioners). The externalisation and co-regulation and safe relationship (therapeutic system/ alliance) provided the safe container to explore this unsafe place a little more without moving outside of the client's window of tolerance – what she could tolerate, without feeling flooded or overwhelmed. We call this Titration – a drop of the 'disturbance' (activation of feeling, memory etc), and not too much."

"Here the practitioner is, as she states, pendulating - tracking the clients window of tolerance, and leaving the 'disturbing' unsafe place before it becomes intolerable or too much to integrate, and heading back to the resourced place – the "safe place" projective representation."

"This is an important part of the role of the horse in EAP- the practitioner can support the client to orient to the horses 'unique feedback' as a unique bio-feedback mechanism and communication, offering the client an opportunity to notice what they feel, heighten awareness in the moment, and then further support themselves."

with clients how horses will seek to return to a state of calm and regulation, and how it can be a great tool for people to notice the horses' behaviours, to heighten awareness and learn about ourselves. Alicia had (over our sessions together) become very interested in when and how this was happening, between herself and the horses.

We took one final walk over to her 'unsafe' object and Lewis the horse leant down and pushed it with his nose, causing it to fall over. Alicia laughed. We then reflected together how Lewis had interacted with and changed the unsafe object, and how Alicia felt it had become less scary for her now.

"Here the role of the horse was to evoke – Lewis evoked a laugh, some joy, lightness or humour into the serious and important themes and psychological processes."

Alicia has a high level of detail in her memory of traumatic events. She explained that they replay over in her memory like a movie. She said the movie that she sees in her mind is in black and white and has the old film border around the edge. She explained that she feels like these movies play over in her mind and she isn't able to stop or pause them.

We spoke about the possibly of a 'remote control' for this 'movie'. She said the remote only has a play button. We spoke about the possibility of creating a 'pause' or 'stop' button on her remote. This aspect needs further therapeutic intervention to help her work through that strategy of finding some control over those memories

"This strategy sounds like it was introduced to support the client to have more intention and control over when and how she processes her memories, keeping her inside her window of tolerance."

returning and creating such physical and psychological disturbance for her. However, today's session appeared to be a good start for Alicia in giving her a concept of how she may manage the movies with a pause or stop, just as we did (literally from horse back) with breathing, returning our attention and moving to the safe place, then, coming back to the unsafe place when she feels ready to give it a little more attention.

REFLECTION

This was our last session for the term. Next term, I am thinking Alicia and I may be able to start some stage two trauma work and exploring her traumatic memories via attending to, re-negotiating, discharging and hopefully completing some of the biological effects of trauma memories.

"Additionally, Peter Levine teaches a practice called memory re-negotiation, that is practiced within the somatic experiencing approach. Here, clients have an opportunity to re-negotiate trauma memories with new information, time, support (to bring in, in polyvagal terms, more ventral into the sympathetic state, of fear and anger from trauma memories). This does not mean the trauma memory is invalidated or unprocessed, on the contrary, after the trauma memory is validated and emotionally processed with expression and meaning-making, the practitioner has the option to explore memory re-negotiation, to build a new brain-body response to the memory, in the here and now. This may be something to explore in the future with this client."

"Yes, psychotherapy takes time, and, trauma requires a whole person approach – including working with the nervous state, biology, somatic expression, emotional, meaning/ cognitive, behavioural and relational approach. Luckily, well-trained EAP practitioners can work at this level quite successfully, integrating horses, animals, nature and movement into psychotherapy."

"

Deep Change happens through Experiencing and Experimenting, not through Intellectualisation and Insight. "

MEG KIRBY

CONCLUSION

Now that you have travelled through all the case studies, you may have noticed many things. Particularly, you may have noticed how the theory (evidently) underpins all of the sessions, and yet how different each session was. I hope so! All sessions have a consistent theory and practice methodology underpinning the work, however, none of the sessions were the same. Each session was a unique matrix that combined an attunement to the individual clients' presentation and needs, and, an inclusion of the practitioners' style, skills and tendencies, the horse's or herd talents, tendencies and behaviour, and the specific facilities, setting and natural environment. All of these client, practitioner, horse and field ingredients co-create and shape the unique feel, content and delivery of each session. This is the art of the work. EPI practitioners deliver a powerful practice that is both a reflection of their authentic expression and yet is truly client-centred. Clients can experience a

psychotherapy or experiential learning session that is tailored to their unique needs. Horses get to be who they are and "show up" in a way that honours their species-specific nature. The natural world sits as the safe container, resourcing, connecting and nourishing all. AWARE Therapy™ is an incredibly powerful and effective psychotherapy and experiential learning process, that supports humans, animals, and the natural world, to learn, heal and change together....for the good of all. I hope you have enjoyed this exposé in "equine therapy" and now have a deeper understanding of the wonderful work of The Equine Psychotherapy Institute model of Equine Assisted Psychotherapy and Equine Assisted Learning.

Meg Kirby

BIBLIOGRAPHY

Dana, D. (2018). *The polyvagal theory in therapy: Engaging the rhythm of regulation*. W W Norton & Company.

Fisher, J. (2017). *Healing the fragmented selves of trauma survivors: Overcoming internal self-alienation*. Routledge/Taylor & Francis Group.

Hallberg, L. (2017). *The Clinical Practice of Equine-Assisted Therapy: Including Horses in Human Healthcare* (1st ed.). Routledge.

Heller, L., & LaPierre, A. (2012). *Healing developmental trauma: How early trauma affects self-regulation, self-image, and the capacity for relationship*. North Atlantic Books.

Imel, Z. E., & Wampold, B. E. (2008). *The importance of treatment and the science of common factors in psychotherapy*. In S. D. Brown & R. W. Lent (Eds.), Handbook of counseling psychology (p. 249–266). John Wiley & Sons, Inc.

Joyce, P., & Sills, C. (2018). *Skills in Gestalt counselling & psychotherapy* (4th ed.). SAGE.

Kirby, M. (2016). *An Introduction to Equine Assisted Psychotherapy: Principles, Theory, and Practice of The Equine Psychotherapy Institute Model*. Balboa Press.

Landreth, G. L. (2012). *Play therapy: The art of relationship* (3rd ed.). Routledge/Taylor & Francis Group.

Levine, P. A. (1997). *Waking the tiger: Healing trauma: the innate capacity to transform overwhelming experiences*. North Atlantic Books.

Levine, P. A. (2010). *In an Unspoken Voice: How the Body Releases Trauma and Restores Goodness*. North Atlantic Books.

Levine, P. A. (2015). *Trauma and Memory: Brain and Body in a Search for the Living Past: A Practical Guide for Understanding and Working with Traumatic Memory*. North Atlantic Books.

Ogden, P., Minton, K., & Pain, C. (2006). *Trauma and the body: A sensorimotor approach to psychotherapy.* W. W. Norton & Company.

Perry, B. D. (2007). *The Boy Who Was Raised as a Dog: and Other Stories from a Child Psychiatrist's Notebook – What Traumatised Children Can Teach Us About Life, Loss and Healing.* Ingram Publisher Services US.

Porges, S. W. (2017). *Norton series on interpersonal neurobiology. The pocket guide to the polyvagal theory: The transformative power of feeling safe.* W W Norton & Co.

Siegel, D. J. (2010). *Mindsight: The new science of personal transformation.* Bantam Books.

Siegel, D. J. (2020). *The Developing Mind: How Relationships and the Brain Interact to Shape Who We Are* (3rd ed.). The Guilford Press.

PHOTOGRAPHY CREDITS

Page 3: Anne Simpson | Pink Turtle Photography | www.pinkturtlephotography.com.au

Page 4: Anne Simpson | Pink Turtle Photography | www.pinkturtlephotography.com.au

Page 5: Anne Simpson | Pink Turtle Photography | www.pinkturtlephotography.com.au

Page 6: Michelle Van Kampen

Page 10: Helena Lopes | instagram.com/helena_wlt/

Page 13: Gary Chambers

Page 16: Annie Spratt | anniespratt.com

Page 23: Sabina Sturzu | unsplash.com/@sabinasturzu

Page 27: Anne Simpson | Pink Turtle Photography | www.pinkturtlephotography.com.au

Page 30: Ainslie Gilles-Patel | ainsliegillespatel.com

Page 32: Helena Lopes | instagram.com/helena_wlt/

Page 34: Milk & Milo Photography

Page 44: Parsing Eye | unsplash.com/@parsingeye

Page 46: Malek Jamal | unsplash.com/@maleksphotos

Page 55: Kelly Forrister | unsplash.com/@kellyforrister

Page 56: Joseph Daniel | unsplash.com/@joseph_h

Page 58: Genevieve Gittoes

Page 70: Soledad Lorieto | unsplash.com/@sool_lorieto

Page 72: Briannagh Clare | instagram.com/briannagh.clare

Page 83: Irina Kajdakowska | pexels.com/@irina-kajdakowska-1499131

Page 84: Soledad Lorieto | unsplash.com/@sool_lorieto

Page 86: Cailin Rose | www.cailinrose.com

Page 94: Oscar Nilsson | oscr.se

Page 96: Dorota Kudyba | instagram.com/kudybadorota

Page 98: Jaslyn Rose Photography

Page 106: Alex Blajan | unsplash.com

Page 108: Finding Grace Photography

Page 120: Zoltan Tasi | instagram.com/zoltan_tasi

Page 130: Mat Reding | instagram.com/matreding

Page 132: Milena Dna | behance.net/milenadenarvaez

Page 134: Briannagh Clare | instagram.com/briannagh.clare

Page 144: Timur Kozmenko | instagram.com/timrael

Page 146: Jaslyn Rose Photography

Page 156: Steppinstars | pixabay.com

Page 160: Anne Simpson | Pink Turtle Photography | www.pinkturtlephotography.com.au

Printed in the USA
CPSIA information can be obtained
at www.ICGtesting.com
LVHW081420251023
762060LV00063B/476